IN HARMONY WITH NATURE

CREATIVE COUNTRY CONSTRUCTION

IN HARMONY

WITH NATURE

CREATIVE COUNTRY CONSTRUCTION

Christian Bruyére • Robert Inwood

DRAKE PUBLISHERS INC · NEW YORK · LONDON

Published in 1975 by
Drake Publishers, Inc.
381 Park Avenue South
New York, New York 10016

Library of Congress Cataloging in Publication Data

Bruyere, Christian
  IN HARMONY WITH NATURE

    1. Country life.   I. Title
S521.B86   640   74-22581
ISBN 0-87749-778-8
ISBN 0-87749-779-6 (Paperback)

Printed in the United States of America.

Printing   3 4 5 6 7 8 9

CONTENTS

IN HARMONY
WITH NATURE

CREATIVE COUNTRY CONSTRUCTION

From Many Creeks
flows A River

There we were on top of it all, sitting at our picture window, sipping cocktails in our plush, highrise apartment in the heart of a huge eastern city. The 15,000 people residing on our block shared its conveniences, but very few of us even cared to pass the time of day with each other. We felt like bees in a filing cabinet anonymously struggling for the betterment of the hive. We were servants to the protective security it offered us.

To maintain our personal sanity in that situation we surrounded ourselves with hundreds of material conveniences. There had to always be an immediate reminder that what we were sacrificing, healthwise and emotionally, was being compensated for by the pleasure we received from the manufactured world which surrounded us.

Our greatest enjoyment came when my wife and I were lucky enough to share the same day-off together. Then we'd jump in our sports car and join the multitudes, who also found it necessary to periodically escape from the noise and pollution of urban life. And after several hours of driving, we found peace in secluded, forested spots, beside small clear-water lakes. There we'd picnic and skinny dip. We'd forget our cares and appreciate the natural beauty of the place. We'd lay on the tall grass and smell the pine-scented, refreshing air. We felt more comfortable and secure there than in the locked confines of our expensive apartment. But always too soon, the bee-hive summoned us to return.

We began craving those carefree excursions into the country. Thoughts of actually changing our life-style began to dominate our spare moments. We spent two years reading available information about living in the woods and preparing a homestead which would provide us with food and shelter. In that period we realized how important it was to find a place of our own. A place where the sounds we heard would be the flowing of creeks, chirping of birds, and the whistling of the wind through the trees instead of the roaring of subways, honking of horns, and the hollering of poorly matched married couples blaming one another for their torment.

We searched for a long time, and we finally found a piece of land to our liking. Though the searching was very enjoyable, and put us in touch with many fine people who were living the style we wanted to, it left us short of cash. We had just enough money to buy the land and rent a small cabin until we could build our own house. I found a job at the local mill, in order to raise the money we needed for our supplies. For months, I sweated on the "green chain", lifting wet boards and transfering them from one place to another. For some strange reason, though, I rather enjoyed that job. It readied me for the hard work I had ahead of me on my own homestead. It also put me in touch with several of the local people who were later very instrumental in the construction of my house. In fact, a few of those fellow mill workers have become my closest friends and working companions.

We bought our place in February, but we didn't really get started with the building of the house until late spring. Those first few months were filled with planning on the layout of the homestead. Before we made any decisions of placement, we had to prune some of the wild growth so we'd know what the area looked like.

I took on the chore of limbing each tree in our thick, six-acre forest. I cut off every branch as high up as I could reach with an axe (plate 1). This may sound like a lot of work, but it was very satisfying. By limbing the trees in that manner, I opened up the forest and turned it into a park with many paths and walkways. I also became sensitive to the land and looked forward to every task on it with a zen-like enthusiasm. I knew I was where I wanted to be.

As far back as February, we watched the arch of the sun. We wanted the house positioned so that in the cold winter the kitchen and dining areas received the warm morning sun through the windows. It was also important that the hot summer sun's arch be in such a position that the sunlight would be blocked by the roof eaves and not enter those areas.

After much experimentation, we finally located a site for the house that would provide proper sunlight. We kept this site completely surrounded by trees to keep it cool in the summer and make it warmer in the winter. Trees are a natural wind breaker that shield an area from the icy winter winds. Before we staked off the exact house sight, we made sure to cut down any snags or standing dead trees which might possibly fall on the structure we would build. Every Cottonwood tree was also removed because this species has a weak root structure and

Cottonwoods have been known to fall for no apparent reason (plate 2).

1

COTTONWOOD

2

The area we chose was also well out of sight of the public road, but close enough to it to be practical in winter. We have no problem carrying our groceries and supplies down the short path to the house, yet we are not assaulted by car lights and constant road noises.

Long before we actually started construction, we put stakes around the proposed perimeter of the house. And every morning we came to the site from our nearby tent and inspected that area. Some mornings the area would seem very tiny, so we would enlarge the perimeter. Other mornings the area would seem huge. Those mornings we'd make it smaller. We soon began "playing house" in the area. We figured out where the various sections would be and how much space would be necessary for each. In the kitchen we measured areas for refrigerator, stove, sink, cabinets, and cupboards.

Then Janey would pretend to make a meal. I'd "go in the livingroom, stoke the fireplace, and sit down on the couch." I'd pretend to entertain friends. We'd pass each other in the hallway and sit down in the diningroom to eat. Though we didn't stick to plan for the finished product, we had a good idea of the space we needed. It turned out that 20' x 24' with an adequate loft area would be sufficient space for us—no immediate plans for enlarging our family.

We wanted a house where the rooms were defined by layout of furniture, not by walls and partitions. In conventional houses the kitchen is separated from the livingroom and other areas. If a conversation was happening in the livingroom, the cook in the kitchen could not participate in it because of the space barriers. We are gregarious people, and we like being with others—so we eliminated partitions on the bottom floor. The only separate space is the mudroom area to keep out drafts.

After we set up the batter boards to make sure the 20' x 24' area was square, I dug 20 holes, four rows of five, for the cement piers which would hold up the sills. There wasn't any span greater than 6' in any direction between them. I felt it was necessary to have that many piers so as to prevent the floor from sagging and to make sure the foundation was good and solid. It's a real drag to have to reinforce a poorly planned foundation as an afterthought.

Each of the holes for the piers was about 2½' deep and was wide enough for the forms which framed the 6" x 6" piers. The frostline was only 18" below the surface, but the soil was clay and was not as stable as rock or other porous soils. Because of this factor we had to dig an additional 1' to support the piers on a firmer sand-type soil. The piers stuck out above the ground about 10" to prevent the sill logs from coming in contact with the clay soil.

We used a mixture of 5 parts clean sand and 1 part Portland Cement for the piers. Many larger rocks and pieces of scrap metal were tapped into the concrete to save on cement and add to the strength of the mixture (plate 3).

3

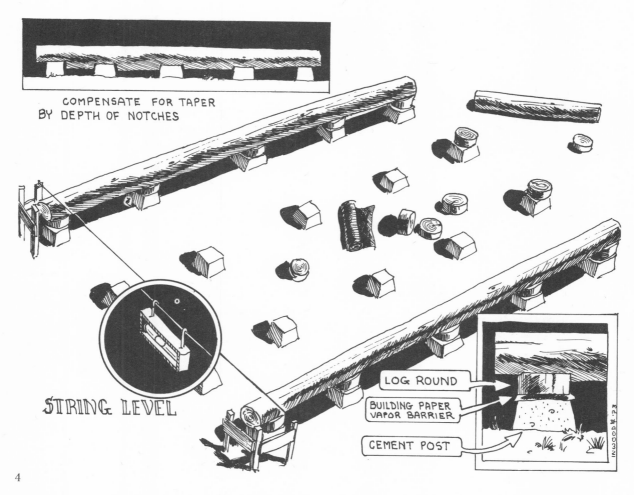

COMPENSATE FOR TAPER
BY DEPTH OF NOTCHES

STRING LEVEL

LOG ROUND

BUILDING PAPER
VAPOR BARRIER

CEMENT POST

4

The area was relatively level, but there was a slight difference in height among the finished piers. These differences in height were made up by various lengths of log-rounds which were set above the piers. Small squares of black building paper were then placed between the log-rounds and the piers. They acted as vapour barriers to protect the logs against the dampness of the concrete.

The four sill logs were notched in place. The two outer sills were dealt with first. They were raised to the height of two string-levels, and both ends were notched onto the pier rounds. The depths of the notches were determined by the log's relationship to the other sills. The notches made them level with each other. If the log being worked was higher than the other sills already in place, its notch was

made as deep as necessary until the sill was lowered to the height of the others. The space between the sills and the ground is being used for storage (plate 4).

Before we went any further on the construction of the house, we dug out the drainage system. Because the soil is clay and does not allow for proper drainage, we had to dig a deep dry well which is 8' wide, 10' long, and 12' deep. This hole is located about 5' east of the kitchen and shower areas. It is far enough from the house to prevent flooding the foundation piers, but it is close enough to save on expensive drainage pipe.

After the drainage system was dug out, we refilled 9' of it with many pick-up truck loads of large rocks. The bigger the better, for drainage. An end of the 2″ plastic drain pipe was placed above the

In Harmony with Nature   7

rocks, then the hole was covered with large cedar logs. A layer of 2″ boards and a black building-paper vapour barrier were placed above the logs, then a final covering of dirt was shoved over the other materials to protect this system. (plate 5). For additional foundation support, and to seal off the area under the sills so cold air wouldn't come through from under the floor, we built a rock retaining wall around the perimeter of the house. For this wall, I dug an 18″-wide and 2½′-deep hole between the outer piers. The bottom of the hole was filled with 4″ of mortar, 3 parts sand and 1 part masonry cement. The masonry cement when dry, produces a white finish which is more appealing to me than the darker finish of regular cement. It also takes less time to dry.

groove cedar, which was on sale at the local mill. After the subfloor was nailed in place, 4″ thick strips of fiberglas insulation was stapled under the floor joists, leaving a dead air space between the insulation and the subfloor. Care should be taken when installing the insulation. If the fiberglas is not properly sealed, the 4″ space between it and the subfloor will be a wind tunnel instead of a dead air space.

To make sure it is sealed properly, overlap the ends of the paper backing whenever possible and make sure to cover the open joist ends. Though there is zero heat loss through the floor, this area must be well protected to prevent cold air from entering (plate 8).

One of the subtle room divisions that we designed is an 11″ high raised platform

5

6

Large rocks were then fitted into the wet mixture, and other rocks were mortared over them until the wall sealed off the area between the ground and the sill logs. The rocks touching the sills were wedged in for a tight fit and a 5′ space was left at the west wall for a store entrance (plate 6).

The 2 x 8 floor joists were then placed over the sills at 16″ centers (plate 7). A subfloor was put in over these joists. This subfloor is of low grade, 2 x 8 tongue and

FLOOR JOISTS

7

for the dining area. It is roughly a 9 x 12 area which is longer at the south wall than in the inside (plate 9). The height of the raised area was determined by what we considered a comfortable step up.

In the early spring, long before we began the foundation, I went out searching for logs for the stockade type walls. A farmer up the road wanted some acreage cleared for a pasture. He told me to tell everyone who wanted firewood or logs for building that they were welcome to cut on his property, the wood was free for the taking. I told everyone I knew about the place, and before long all the usable timber was cleared away. My first plan was to cut down live trees and buck them to 7' lengths, then to peel off their barks and let them dry a season. But when I arrived at the site I came upon a pile of aged, fallen timbers. They were mostly pine, tamarack, and fir. By the end of the day we transported enough logs home to do all the walls. I was really pleased with my find.

Since the logs were already aged, I could use them immediately. They were light to handle and I wouldn't have to worry about any drastic shrinkage. One thing I didn't figure though, was the problem of peeling aged logs. After

SEALING OFF THE OUTSIDE ENDS

FIBREGLASS FILLS 2"×6" CHANNEL

8

9

struggling with a drawknife for many hours and only completing a couple of logs, I decided there must be a better way to get them peeled. I rounded up several peeling spuds and drawknives and invited all the able bodied teenagers in the area to come to my "peeling party". They accepted my invitation, ate my food, drank my wine, and listened to my music, but by the end of the day only a few of my logs had been peeled. In the days that followed, a couple of the more industrious youths peeled most of the remaining logs. I paid them 50¢ a log and believe me it was well worth it to have that chore out of the way.

A lot of the dark pitch from the bark did not come off the logs. At first I thought the discoloration was ugly, but once the walls were up I began liking the effect of the dry peeled texture and the color patterns of the logs (plate 10).

One day, after the subfloor was finished we sat around drinking wine. We were celebrating our achievements to date and were so inspired by what we had already completed that we soon began the walls. We nailed the 2 x 6 bottom wall plates in place then set up boards outside each of the four perimeters of the foundations. There were actually long batter boards which were mailed into the sills. Each of these eight 2 x 4's extended upright over 7' so a string could be attached near its top. The boards were positioned so the guide strings would be half-a-log's thickness, or 3" inside the perimeter of the building. This would make the strings intersect half a log's diameter at every corner. These points of intersection would designate the exact center of the corner log.

A black line was then drawn along the center of the 2 x 6 bottom-wall plate. A log was centered over this plate. To make sure the upright wall-log was exactly plumb, I attached a weighted string to

10

one of the intersecting strings which crossed above the log. A fishing sinker was used to hold this vertical string plumb. The wall-log was adjusted according to the plumbness of the string. It was then braced with a diagonal board and the weighted string was transferred to the intersecting corner to check the other side of the wall-log. The log was again braced, and was considered to be plumb (plate 11).

When dealing with logs it is very inaccurate to check the plumbness of an upright with a level. No log is perfectly straight from end to end unless it has been hewned or milled that way. All logs have protrusions and low spots. What may be level in one 3'-section does not necessarily give a true reading for the entire length of a log. I had doubts about my simple plumb-reading until I saw the electrical company setting up our power pole. They put it upright with all their expensive equipment, but had to do a final check with a string and a bolt which they suspended from a stick beside the pole.

By the end of the day, we had one log up. It protruded from the flat subfloor like the monolith from "2001." There was something spiritual about that log and what it represented to us. We didn't put up another wall log for days after. We did other chores instead and just marveled at our "monolith," with the forest background.

The following wall logs went up quite fast. Each of the corner logs were put in place and checked for plumbness. Each was to be nailed to the bottom wall plates with 7" ardox nails. One nail on the inside and one on the outside. Ardox nails were used because of their incredible holding ability. The only frustrating thing about them is having to pull them out in case of mistake; forget it. Each

corner log was then braced with diagonal 2 x 4's.

I laminated two 2 x 6 top plates together and nailed them over the corner posts. These double-laminated plates were nailed together every 16", and the nails were staggered to add strength to the plates. An end of each plate was over-lapped to interlock with the intersecting double plates of the corner wall (plate 12).

After the top plates were in place, we filled in the full length wall logs of the west wall, leaving adequate space for the windows. A 3" strip of fiberglas insulation was stapled to the bottom and top plates and along each log. The log to be placed was pushed in as close as possible at the bottom plate by one person, while a second person toenailed it in. We made sure the log was plumb before nailing through the top plate (plate 13).

All the full-length wall logs were put in

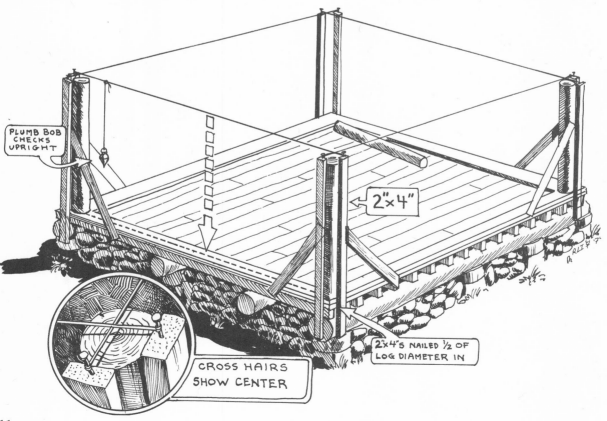

PLUMB BOB CHECKS UPRIGHT

2"x4"

CROSS HAIRS SHOW CENTER

2"x4's NAILED ½ OF LOG DIAMETER IN

place and the window spaces were roughly outlined. To secure the corners and strengthen the walls, 2 x 6 diagonal bracing was used at each corner except for the dining area, or the southwest corner, where it would remain exposed if used. The bracing is hidden in the other corners by a brick wall, a shower stall, and a kitchen stove. These 2 x 6's start at the bottom plates of each wall, a few feet in from the corners and meet at the corners 5′ above the floor. Each are notched into the wall logs (plate 14). The other full-length logs went in by the same manner.

Most of the log structures I've seen in this area have small windows. Their interiors are dull and dingy because not enough light enters to brighten them up. I asked many of the builders of these houses why they wanted such small windows. They all answered me the same. They wanted the small windows to prevent heat loss and to conserve on wood and other heating materials.

We designed our windows big because we wanted light and we desired to view our beautiful homestead. In winter we would be in that house most of the time. I would rather put my energy into cutting an extra cord of wood and have big windows, than to have to spend the winter enclosed by four dingy walls. Anyway, large windows at the south wall bring in more of the sun's heat even during the coldest of winter.

At the west wall we framed a 6' x 4' window space high enough for us to be able to see out of when we are eating. To frame a window when using vertical logs you simply cut your top window header two logs longer so the header log can rest on the vertical sleepers on either side of the opening. Since there is no wall stress on the bottom window sill, it is cut to the size of the window opening and toe nailed to the sleepers on either side. This 2 x 8 sill is tilted downwards towards the outside to shed water which would otherwise collect on it and seep into the house. After the header was nailed in place, short uprights were cut and fitted in the space between it and the top plate. Insulation was then stapled between these short upright studs (plates 15 and 16).

There is a second window at the west wall which is 11" lower than the first. It brings the afternoon light in to the living-room and gives us a view of the forest and the chicken coop (plate 17). On a homestead, it is wise to position your windows

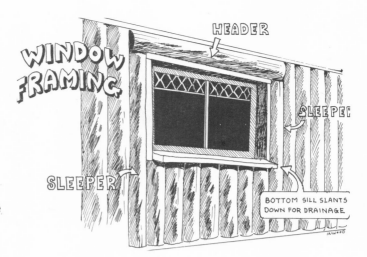

15

16

17

18

so your livestock are in plain view in case of danger.

The north wall has a large window in the center above the wood box. The window is closed off in the winter by a heavy curtain because no sunlight comes in from that direction. Since no sunlight enters from the northwall, it is the coldest wall and should be the most protected. Our Franklin Fireplace is located here. It has a brick wall in back of it to shield the log wall from its heat (plate 18).

Built into the northwall, beside the Franklin Fireplace, is a fire box. It has a large outside entrance at which we load the box full of cord wood. This entrance is covered by a latched door to keep the cold from entering. On the inside, the box has a lid enabling us to take the cord wood out of the box and load it in from the outside. This fire box helps prevent heat loss which would occur if we were opening the door to bring fire wood in. It also keeps the floor clean from the wood chips and pieces of bark which plague many a wilderness housewife's floor (plates 19 and 20).

There is a temporary door at this wall which we used until the main door and front porch had been constructed. This door is very light weight, studded with 2 x 4 and sheathed with cedar 1 x 12's. The main door is at the double log east wall. This wall is double log between the shower room and the kitchen to frame in the mudroom and storage area. We used logs for this purpose because they were a cheap material and went well aesthetically with the other interior design.

The mudroom, which is 5' wide and 11' long, is a necessity for homestead living. It is a separate area where people can enter without disturbing the other occupants of the house with cold draft and noise. It is a place to hang overcoats and take off muddy boots. It is a reorientation corridor to prepare a chilled and road-weary traveler for the warm and cozy indoors. Or to prepare a sedate, wine-filled guest for the journey which awaits him (plate 21).

To save on space, both the inner door to the livingroom and the outer door of the mudroom open towards the outside. The outer door opens to a large enclosed porch which is 6′ wide and 20′ long. It is framed with log and has log rafters which extend 2′ past the porch as eaves (plate 22).

To make the stairs of the raised porch platform, I hewed flat the tops of two log pieces. The first was imbedded in the ground, and the other was perched up 1′ higher than it on log uprights which were buried into the ground.

The south wall has many large windows for heating and lighting purposes. The huge 4′ x 6′ window in the kitchen brightens up that area, so whoever is cooking does not feel trapped in a dingy little space. This window almost makes it seem like we are cooking in an outdoor

20

kitchen. It makes us feel like we are part of the forest which surrounds us instead of closed off from it (plate 23).

For the same light and heat purposes we have two larger 4′ x 4′ windows in the dining area behind the table and two elevated windows in the dormer area above that space. These elevated windows bring in the higher arched summer

19

sun to both the livingroom and dining areas (plate 24).

Also bringing light into these areas are the windows of the west wall. They are very important because they allow the afternoon sunlight, which filters through the tall evergreens, to warm the house and prepare it for the cooler evening.

Though all the window spaces were framed and ready, we did not put in the glass the first year for two main reasons. We wanted to give the walls time to settle and we were running out of money again.

The last task, before the walls were completed, was to cover the insulation strips and seal in between the wall logs. At first I was thinking of cutting out quarter-rounds from larger poles for this purpose, but a nearby friend had a grove of young cedars. He let me thin out the grove and use as many of the narrow poles as I needed for the house. I brought home a truckload and proceeded to peel them. Even though they were green, they were as hard to peel as the dry logs because it was late in the season and the sap was low. But after a few days of constant scraping, they were ready. I beveled the ends of each pole and nailed them into the wall logs tightly over the insulation (plate 25).

With the walls finished, it was time to get started on the loft and roof. I hashed over various roof designs with a few friends who had volunteered their labor and ideas to help us build our house. We decided to cover the kitchen and entry way areas with a bedroom loft and have the area above the livingroom and dining-room open as a high, Cathedral-style ceiling. A 45-degree pitch for the roof seemed to be the best because it made

SHOWER STALL

PORCH

LIVINGROOM

MUDROOM ENTRY WAY

21

22

23

25

24

In Harmony with Nature   17

for a spacious ceiling, allowing a distance of 10′ between the top wall plates and the ridge peak. The 45-degree angle, as we found out while working with it, was the easiest angle to use. Rafters could be simply measured and cut on that angle, and even insulation pieces and sheathing boards for the gable ends could be cut out with the minimal amount of waste and planning.

It was time to begin the loft construction and we did not even have a cross-beam for the joists or a center pole. That problem was quickly taken care of though. A hemlock tree was cut down and two logs were sawed from it. The logs were quickly peeled and brought to the house site. The 7′ log was positioned upright near the center of the floor and the 14′ one was notched in above it. It spanned between that upright and the inner east wall, where it was also notched in place.

26

As we pounded the spikes in, the logs spit back at us.

The longer log extended well past the half way point of the house which was designated as the end of the loft area. Since the pole was longer than necessary, we decided to modify our loft design and add a 36″ extension to the north side of it. This space was used for a book shelf and a reading area. The north end of that additional platform was later closed off for a small linen closet. The loft joists were spaced 16″ on-center and spanned between the north and south walls. Every other 2 x 8 joist was doubled to add support to the loft floor. These doubled joists also acted as braces to prevent the walls from spreading out under the weight of the loft and roof (plate 26).

A subfloor of 2 x 6 fir was nailed across the joists and a finish floor was laid diagonally above it. This diagonal finish floor is another precaution against the walls collapsing. It prevents the stockade walls from twisting by bracing them against leaning in any direction. Some people accuse me of overbuilding, but I don't think I am. I'm just trying to make sure our house stays around for a long time.

Next came the rafters. The rafter sets were put together assembly-line style, using a simple matrix (jig) framework consisting of blocks nailed to the floor. First we laid out one set of rafters and cut their tops at 45-degree angles. The "A" brace was then cut and positioned and the rafter bottoms were notched to fit the top plates. Blocks were nailed around the rafter set in all the necessary places; two at the feet, a few along the sides, and two near the top of each. This method assured us that all the rafters were uniform and it gave us a guide for each of the necessary cuts.

After a few sets of rafters were finished, we laminated two of them together as a double set for the end rafters. One helper stood on the floor with a long board extended, raising the set by the "A" brace, while another helper and I spiked the rafter bottoms to the top wall plates (plate 27).

At this point, Janey and I stood on the loft floor and tried to figure out how much space we would have for our bedroom under that simple gable roof. Neither of us were satisfied. We wanted a larger room. We thought about how some friends of ours turned a small attic space into two good-sized bedrooms by incorporating a large shed dormer into the roof of that structure. We liked the idea and designed our roof to include three shed dormers, one on either side of the bedroom area and one at the south wall just above the dining area, to bring in the morning sunlight to the lower spaces.

We wanted the shed dormers in the bedroom to be 8' wide and we had to be able to stand in them. 5'9" was a good height and came to about a 22-degree pitch. I am glad we stopped long enough to decide on that extra roof space when we did because at that point the dormers were easy to install. At a later time it would involve tearing out rafters or maybe even replacing an already completed roof. We found over and over again that it pays to stop and live in the house at every stage of construction.

All the rafter sets were then spaced at 16" centers and nailed into place. Wherever the rafters braced the ends of the three dormers, they were doubled like the first two sets. The others were single sets. To frame the bedroom dormers, four jack-rafters were cut at 22-degree angles, and each was nailed to a peak of one of the four double rafters. These extending jack-rafters were then supported by several 2 x 4 upright studs spaced 16" apart. At the peak, the jack-rafters were connected by an 8'-double 2 x 6 which spanned between them. Another 8'-double 2 x 6 was then placed between the bottom end of each of the jack-rafters

27

and these headers were braced in the center, between the spaces for windows, by two 2 x 6 uprights (plates 28 and 29).

The livingroom shed dormer was framed in the same manner. Being a smaller dormer, its jack-rafters were cut at 35 degrees. This allowed for a space 8'-long by 2½'-wide in which two windows are going to be put (see plate 24).

After the roof structure and gable ends were framed they were sheathed on the outside with low-grade 1 x 6 hemlock. To protect the roof sheathings from the autumn rains, we covered it with a finish roof of asphalt shingles. Asphalt shingles were chosen because they are safer and last longer than cedar shakes and they are more aesthetic than aluminum. Cedar shakes are more natural and pleasing to the eye, but they are dangerous and are known to ignite with the least little wild spark. In fact a friend of ours this winter lost his house because a spark caught fire to his cedar-shake roof.

With a protective roof over our heads, shielding us from the autumn rain, we turned our energies to the loft interior. Again we stopped and figured out the spaces we needed. For comfortable, uncluttered living, plenty of closets and cupboard space are essential. With our shed-dormer design, there was adequate cupboard area under the dormer windows (plates 30 and 31).

For a closet, we set up a divider wall between the bedroom and what was to be the reading platform. This wall closes off the bedroom from the rest of the house, making it a separate area. The closet space is two-rafters (32″) wide and extends from the north wall to the center crossbeam. It was also partitioned off at the loft doorway entrance.

Because the house is designed for togetherness and has no totally separate spaces except for the mudroom, there is no door to the bedroom, just a heavy

28

29

30

31

velvet drape hung from over the entrance to control heat. When the drape is open it allows the rising heat from downstairs to enter and warm the loft area. When it is closed, it prevents the heat from entering that space.

The inside ceiling of the bedroom and the open Cathedral ceiling were sheathed with 1 x 8 boards, using the lap-siding method. This method was used to prevent having spaces between the boards and to seal off the insulation more efficiently.

Because more heat escapes through roofs than any other section of a structure, I took caution to make sure ours was well insulated with 3½″-thick fiberglas. To find out if our roof had enough insulation, I checked the snow load on it. If the snow melted and iced at the eaves, I knew that heat was escaping. If it stayed on the shingles, the roof was properly dealt with because no heat was escaping to melt it. It is also important to block off the sections between the rafters where they meet the walls. I stuffed loose insulation in those ends and nailed on 15″-board sections to protect the fiberglas.

To figure out a set of stairs for the loft, I first positioned the temporary ladder at various angles to find out which degree of incline would be the most comfortable. An angle of about 45-degrees seemed to be about the best. I put up two 3″-diameter rails at that angle and made notches in them at about every 16″ on-center for the 2½″-diameter pole steps. The rail on the right was longer and extended 3′ above the loft floor to enable the climber to make a graceful entry onto the loft platform in whatever condition he or she might be (see plate 26).

Since we have completed the basic construction of the house and have become familiar with it, we have been finding ourselves preoccupied with putting various finishing touches on it to make it a visible representation of our

personalities. We are making much of the furniture out of log pieces to complement the house's natural setting. The diningroom table was built out of extra 2″ cedar boards. And wherever we found bargains on usable materials, we would contemplate how we could incorporate such finds in our home. For instance, as I was driving into a nearby town this winter, I spotted a stack of broken chimney tiles in front of a builder's supply store. I stopped and asked the store manager what he was going to do with those tile pieces. He told me they fell off a delivery truck and asked me what I intended to do with them. Instead of telling him that I wanted to use them to tile my kitchen floor, I told him I needed them for something less aesthetic so he would give me a better deal of them. He told me I could have them all if I would clear them out from in front of his store. I took the many pieces of the used-to-be 12″ x 12″ chimney tiles and carefully tapped the curved ends with a hatchet blade to flatten them out. There turned out to be enough pieces to cover our kitchen floor. I then bought some ready-mix and mortared them in. I found out, for best results, the tiles should be kept free from moisture when they are being laid because they adhere better when they are dry. So for the price of two 60-pound bags of ready-mix, we now have a beautiful tile kitchen floor (plate 32).

I also want to mention our wood stove for those who are handy, or who have friends who are handy, with a welding torch. This oil-drum stove was made by a friend. It is very efficient, even holds its fire over night. Its flat top makes an excellent for cooking surface, and it uses a lot less wood for the amount of heat it puts out than the Franklin stove (plates 33 and 34).

Now, after just a few months working on our homestead, we are a lifetime away from our plush city apartment and the bee hive which surrounded it. We've made a home for ourselves, complete with aesthetic beauty and spacial comfort. It is surrounded by nature's wonders and a community of people who believe in working and learning together. Our house is just one of the many examples in this immediate area of what can be achieved through cooperation. It was built and designed by a few people who each had a little specialized knowledge and unselfishly shared that collection of information. Without the assistance of those fine people I doubt that this last winter would have been as comfortable as it was, and I am positive that with the practical experience and technical know-how I had when the building was started, we would not be living in a house that we are so proud of. We not only built a house, we built confidence in our own resourcefulness. We also built many lasting friendships with people like ourselves who value the importance of making their needs known and who are always willing to help their fellow man (plate 35).

32

33

34

35

We were living in a small flat in a large west coast city when my wife Kathrina announced that she was pregnant. The thought of parenthood and all its responsibilities sparked a new light in me. I suddenly began to recognize a previously dormant need for security. We both wanted to settle somewhere and have a HOME we could call our own.

We decided to buy an old house just outside the city limits and fix it up for an investment. The house, with payments, tax, and insurance was costing us over $250 a month, but that wasn't so bad since I was clearing over $800. As we started fixing up the house, we began realizing the sad shape it was in. The plumbing was rusted out and leaking, the wiring was dangerous, the whole thing needed much repair. What really got us though was good old compound interest. Out of the $190 a month payments, only $37 of that was going to the principal. At that rate, we would be paying the house off for the next 33 years. Even with all those hassles, we still thought it a good investment and we would not have any trouble getting a good price for it when we decided to sell. But even from the very beginning for some reason this house never really seemed like home.

The property was surrounded by a beautiful wooded area that provided us with nearby peace and serenity—two conveniences rarely found so close to a city. As we considered this asset, so did someone else. Soon, a logging company came in and carelessly wiped out our little neighboring forest. What used to be a wooded playground, was transformed into a graveyard of slash and stumps. We luckily unloaded the property for a little above what we paid for it and decided to look elsewhere for a home.

Some friends of ours were thinking about undeveloped rural land. They heard about a place that was near a large lake and was surrounded by picturesque mountains. We were into taking a vacation in that direction, so we offered to go see the place for them. We went to the area but it was still early spring, and because of the muddy runoffs we could not get up the road which led to that parcel of land. The valley we were in was so incredibly beautiful that we decided to inquire around to find out what else was available.

We soon found just the place we wanted. It was bordered on one side by a large river, on another side by a rapid flowing creek. It was deep within a thick forest of second growth. This land and the immediate area that surrounded it had been logged out many years ago and was left forgotten. We camped near the river and stayed until the mosquitoes finally drove us out. But they didn't stop us from returning.

We came back with our friends and found that they shared our enthusiasm. Within a few weeks we made a deal for the land and bought it. Throughout the next few months I spent as much time as

I could in the library learning about architectural design. I had visions of the home I wanted to build. It was an arch shaped house with a courtyard in front. I was preoccupied by this vision because I had never really had a home before, not even as a child.

On returning to our land when we felt prepared enough to do so, we set up a tent and waited for the rains to stop. It rained for several weeks. We put up a quick "A"-frame to shelter us from the miserable weather. As we finished the roof, the sun came out and shone for seven weeks straight. Kathrina and I spent many days walking around our section of the property, trying to decide where we were going to build our home. We wanted to be near the river and we wanted to have a southwest exposure so we could get as much sunlight as possible.

Kathrina put markers up in a line, designating where the sun rose over the mountains on a certain date (May 1). She put another set showing where the sun set on that date. From these markers we calculated how much sunlight we would have at a given spot in the different seasons of the year. In May, the sun's arch was still pretty low, so if a site received plenty of sunlight at that time of year, it would receive even more when the sun's arch was at its peak in the summer. After several trials, we finally located the ideal building site.

While I was working on the plans for the house, I also figured out the quantities of lumber we would need. I checked the local mills and priced the boards. Prices are always on the rise and materials are not always available. I knew that in order to get the best deal, I had to act immediately.

At that time I did not know anyone in the valley except for our partners in the land. I went out looking for a caterpillar to make a road into our property. As I

was searching, I met many fine people especially the man with the "cat". I asked him to do the work for me and I would pay him what he asked, but he said he had hurt his back and could not do it. I knew how to operate his machine, so asked if I could borrow it. It never hurts to ask; and a person doesn't get what he needs unless he makes his needs known. To my surprise, he let me use his machine. I made the road and returned the "cat" to him. I told him that I used it for 15 hours. He saw the road and said that it couldn't have taken that long. He asked me for $20 for the use of the "cat." I couldn't believe his generosity. Here was a man who was unspoiled by greed; a man who genuinely liked people and wasn't out to get all he could from them.

As I searched for a truck to haul the lumber, I met a family of people who were just as helpful as that man. Instead of making an impersonal bargain of renting a truck for cash, Kathrina and I traded our labor for the use of that vehicle. We worked in their nursery, and we learned much useful information from these experienced homesteaders who unselfishly traded their knowledge and good "vibes" for our respect and friendship. That was one of the best deals I've ever made. We are still reaping the benefits.

Whenever I had time to spare, I went around and searched out more of the local inhabitants. Never have I met so many compassionate people who were willing to share themselves so freely. (Sure there were a few grumps and such, but there's no need to mention them). Most of the folks here have two things in common: the willingness to communicate their needs and knowledge and the awareness that such communication is a vital element of their existence.

In these local travels I also met a fellow who was building his house out of scrap lumber. I asked him where he was getting the material. He showed me an old lumber mill that was being torn down. The owners were going to set fire to it soon, but they allowed anyone who wanted to salvage what they could use to take what they needed. By the time I got there, all the usable 2″ material had been stripped off. I walked around, feeling disappointed—I missed the boat. Then I realized, there beside me was a huge 23″ long 8 x 12 truss beam. Near it were several other large timber pieces that had been left to be burned. There were 8 x 8's, 10 x 12', 4 x 4's, and 6 x 6's. Altogether, we got six pickup-truck loads from there.

Shortly after that, we found an old planer mill that had caved in from age and left discarded. The owners let us dismantle it and take what we needed. Then, a few days later, the railroad was rebuilding an old trestle and was going to burn the old timbers. We loaded the timbers up and took them home.

Before long, we had a mountain of such timbers. We measured everything and made a list of what we had. I then tried to figure out how we could best utilize the material in our carefully thought-out plan. The timbers could not be efficiently figured into the plan. Many of the pieces were too short, and the nice, long ones would have to be cut. So the original plan was thrown out, and a new one was drawn up on the basis of the lengths we had. The dimensions of the house were changed in order to prevent wasting any of the long beams. The west wall, originally 20'-long, was changed to 23', the length of the longest timber I found. The north wall stayed 20', the east wall became 16', and the south wall became 21'. So the house took on a shape of a trapezoid instead of its original shape.

Because of the massiveness and structural soundness of the timbers, I discarded the frame construction techniques that I studied for so long and decided to use the post-and-beam method. The post-and-beam method would give the walls more structural strength and would prevent having to clutter the house with all the interior upright supports our original plan called for.

It was already late in June before we started our foundation. Since the property is all level river-front land, we didn't have to deal with a slope. We were free to pick the best site on the basis of sun exposure and view of the river. Instead of having a foundation wall around the perimeter of the building, I chose to use a network of sill logs which would be supported on 9 cement piers. The cedar logs were mill runaways given to me by a neighbor who had snagged them out of the river as they flowed downstream from the local mill.

I laid out the position of the foundation with traditional batter boards and checked the trueness of the two square corners in the same manner as explained in other chapters. If those corners were true, so would the others be. At this point I checked the levelness of the ground with a surveyor's level that I borrowed. Then the holes for the foundation piers were dug. A hole 2'-wide and 2'-deep was dug at each corner, in the center of each side, and in the center of the building. These holes were well below the 18″ frost line.

The bottom pad of each pier is 24″-square and 6″-high. These pads were poured first, without forms. A 48″-long rebar rod was then stuck into the pads (plate 1). When the pads were nearly dry, 1x cedar boxes that were 12″-square and 33″ in length were centered over the pads. Concrete was then shoveled into the boxes until each was filled. When the concrete set, the boxes were removed. Each pier stuck up 15″ above the ground to lift the sill logs well above the carpenter ants. It is said that these little devils won't

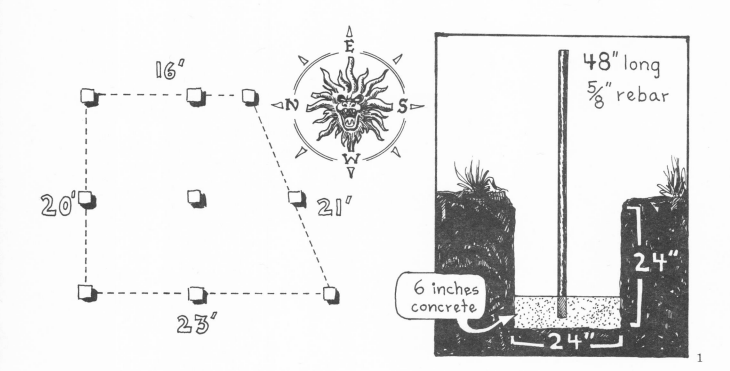

16'

20'

21'

23'

48" long
5/8" rebar

6 inches
concrete

24"

24"

climb over 18" of concrete to make their nests. The rebar pin extended far enough above the pier to go through the cedar sill beams and go about 4" into the upright posts which rested on them (plate 2).

The sill logs ranged between 9"-to-14" in diameter. They were each notched so there were 8" of beam above the piers to make them level. The larger diameter butt-ends were placed directly on the piers and were then notched on both top and bottom to prevent too much from being taken out for one notch. You can cut up to a quarter of a given log's thickness for each notch without weakening that beam and losing the structural value of the material. If more than a quarter of its diameter is cut out there is a tendency for the log to split lengthwide under pressure (plate 3). I tenon-notched the thickest beams over the piers and lapped the perpendicular sills so they would fit over them. A hole was then drilled in each end to accommodate the rebar pins which would secure them together (plate 4).

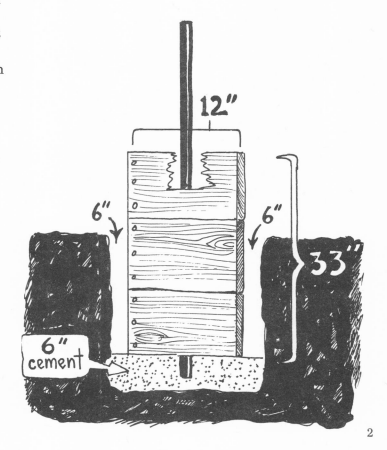

12"

6"

6"

33"

6"
cement

3

4

Rebar sunk into concrete post extends up thru both sill logs

Never cut off more than ¼ round on the underside

← ¾" bit

Since I was working alone most of the time, I had an incredible amount of difficulty moving the first few beams. Such physical punishment just didn't seem necessary. I thought about various simple machines which could help me in my work. I remembered coming upon a mountain stream in my travels. This stream was being mined by hand, gold-rush style. There were pyramids of rocks piled on the banks; some of those rocks were huge boulders. They were taken out of the stream bed and piled on the banks in order to get to the stream's gravel bed. I asked an old prospector how they moved those stones up in such high piles. He told me about the gin-pole device they had used which consisted of a stationary support pole and a swinging pole that was notched into its butt. The swinging gin pole's tip was suspended out in a 45-degree angle by a guy wire which was secured near the top of the stationary pole. A come-along, or a block-and-tackle, was attached to the tip of the pole to lift the huge rocks. The swinging pole was then guided to the bank by ropes. If there was a substantial tree around, it was used as the support pole. If not, a scissor (a two-member tripod) was made out of two logs and it was latched together at the top. The scissor was held almost upright, leaning a bit toward the stream, by a guy wire which was attached to a solid stump or tree in the background. A block-and-tackle was then suspended down from the peak of the scissor into the water. The block-and-tackle line was then guided to the bank by hand and the boulder was lowered to the pile. This second method was less efficient than the first, but it prevented many an aching back.

From my stationary pole, I used a 50′ Cottonwood which was beside the building site. The tree was going to be felled anyway, so I cut a deep wedge shaped notch into its butt for the seat of the swinging pole. The butt of the 35'-tamarack swinging pole was trimmed and put into the notch. It was suspended at a 45-degree angle toward the house site with a guy wire secured to the stationary pole about 10' above the notch. This gin pole was later used for the roof's ridgepole.

A chain block was hung from the swinging pole's tip, and a pair of log tongs was attached to the end of the tackle to grip the log or beam. I soon found the tongs to be a dangerous and inefficient method of gripping the logs because they only secured them at one center-balance point. I ended up using a chain that circled the log at two points and was lifted in the middle by the traveling block's hook. This pole could swing in a 150-degree radius and could reach any part of the building site. When this device was in action I could pick up the biggest log or beam, crank it up, swing it into position with guide ropes and lower it down to where I wanted it. This was a slow process, because of the time it took to raise and lower the beams with the chain block, but there was nothing difficult about it and there was no back-breaking by the lifting that had to be done (plate 5).

5

GIN POLE

After the sill logs were in place, the 2 x 8 floor joists were put in across them, running east and west. Though they were about 20′ in length, they never spanned more than 8′ between supporting points. A good rule to follow when putting in floor joists is to make sure the joists are at least 1″-thick per-foot of span. If the joists span 8′, you need to use 2 x 8's. Actually this is more substantial than houses in the city are built, but most city houses nowadays are not worth the mortgage they are written on.

To allow for a split-level main floor which would be a subtle divider between the living area and the dining-kitchen areas, I hewed the inside of the west wall sill and the side of the center sill that faced it. These surfaces were made flat to accommodate the double 2 x 4 lips which were spiked to the bottom of these sides. The lower joists of the dining and kitchen areas were notched over these lips to split the level of the floor. The joists for the upper level were then nailed in over the crossing sills, making that floor 8″ higher than the lower one.

The 1 x 12 cedar subfloor was then put down so we would have a nice surface to work on. All the flooring was nailed on with ardox, spiral-type nails to keep it from squeeking. This type of nail prevents floor squeeking because it holds better and does not have a tendency to pull away from the joists as the floor is being used (plate 6).

The 8 upright support posts were put in above the sills, over the outlining piers. A hole was first drilled in each of their bottom ends for the 4″-long rebar which stuck out above the sills. The four corner posts were 10 x 10's that were salvaged from the planer mill and the four inside posts were 8 x 8's that were runners for the carriage in the old saw mill. They were

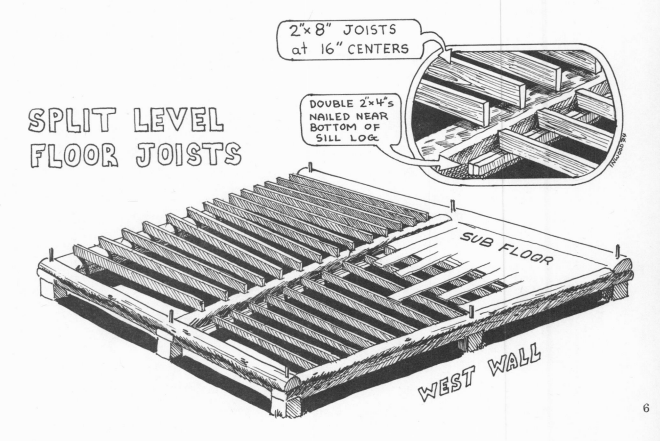

2″ x 8″ JOISTS at 16″ CENTERS

DOUBLE 2″ x 4′s NAILED NEAR BOTTOM OF SILL LOG

SPLIT LEVEL FLOOR JOISTS

SUB FLOOR

WEST WALL

6

sawed on two sides. The sawed sides were used as flat surfaces for the wall logs or lumber frames to rest against. The round sides could be seen from the inside and outside of the building. These fir posts carry all the structural weight. The wall logs or studs do not carry any of it. Each of these posts could support as much as 100 pounds-per-square-inch. So an 8 x 8 has the structural strength to support 6400 pounds above it.

The posts were checked for straightness with a level and were braced with diagonal 2 x 4's. The perimeter beams were then raised with the gin pole and were lowered into position above the posts. The gin pole worked good but it was a slow operation. When the huge 1500-pound beams were lifted in the air with this homemade contraption, we were careful not to get underneath them. We guided the suspended beams with poles and ropes and stood clear until they were in position (plate 7).

The ends of the beams and tops of the posts were notched and a deep hole was augered into each of the ends. Steel pins were then driven into each of these joining corners to secure them. The steel pins are lengths of 1/2″ and 5/8″ bar stock that I found in a local junk yard. Most of this material was tie bolts out of an old boiler which I hacksawed to length. These super hard steel rods were only 5 cents per pound and were a lot stronger than the softer rebar stock and much cheaper (plate 8).

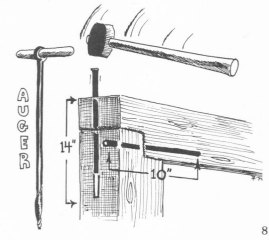

8

7

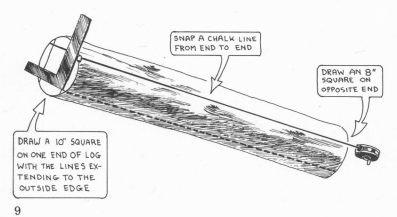

SNAP A CHALK LINE FROM END TO END

DRAW AN 8" SQUARE ON OPPOSITE END

DRAW A 10" SQUARE ON ONE END OF LOG WITH THE LINES EXTENDING TO THE OUTSIDE EDGE

9

SCORE ALONG CHALK LINES WITH CHAIN SAW

10

SHIPBUILDER'S ADZ

11

Next came the cedar-log centerpost to brace the ceiling beams. This was my first attempt at hewing a log on four sides. I wanted to eventually carve the pole and make it an ornamental finishing touch to the house. To start the hewing process, I centered a 10″ square on one end of the log and an 8″ square on the opposite end, letting all the crossing lines go out to the edge of the ends. A chalk line was snapped down the length of the log from one line to its corresponding line on the opposite end. With a chainsaw, I then made a series of scoring cuts into the side of the log to the depth of the lines (plates 9 and 10).

After one side was scored, the log was dogged in place and the sections between the cuts were knocked out. This technique was repeated on each side, and the whole log was trimmed with a ship-builder's adze (plate 11).

Instead of raising the log so the 10″-square end was down, I put that larger end up to give the centerpost a tapering effect, making the building seem lighter. This effect would be even more pronounced if the centerpost were longer (plates 12 and 13).

The four center 8 x 8 ceiling beams were put in and joined over the centerpost. Each beam spanned only from the center of the wall to the top of the centerpost. I found out later that this was a structural error. Because the separate pieces joined in the center istead of making a continuous tie across the house, this design lacked sheer strength. Sheer strength is the tieing together of the separate parts of a whole section to reinforce it. For example, in order to gain the greatest amount of sheer strength when tieing a wall together, the sheathing boards should be put on diagonally. The diagonals create several triangles, which is the strongest form of sheer bond. If the ceiling beams were two continuous pieces

12

13

notched over the centerpole instead of four separate sections, their sheer strength would be considerably stronger because they would in fact tie the walls together. Other ceiling beams were then put in as braces for the 2 x 4 joists which span the three loft sections of the roof area.

The 2 x 4 loft-floor joists were nailed in at 16″ centers above the ceiling beams and a floor of 1 x 6 tongue-and-groove was fitted together over the joists. I used tongue-and-groove stock because a subfloor is not necessary with this interlocking material. No dust comes through between the boards, falling to the lower sections of the house. And with the joists at 16″ centers, this 1x flooring is sturdy enough not to bounce or sag with weight (plate 14).

We did not want a full second story, but we did want a loft space built into the sloping roof. The only way to have a full, open space between the ceiling and roof, without cluttering that space with a network of roof trusses, is to support the rafters at the peak with a ridgepole. The ridgepole ties the rafter tops together and braces them. This prevents the rafters from sagging under a heavy snow load and spreading the walls with an outward force of pressure resulting from the collapsing rafters.

Because of the structural importance the ridgepole has in this type of design, it has to be a good-size log at least 8″-to-12″ in diameter. Our ridgepole is the 35′ tamarack which had served us well as the gin pole. We just lowered it on to the loft floor and disconnected it from the stationary cottonwood tree. 5′ was then sawn off its tip to make it 30′ long to provide 5′ overhangs on either side to keep the walls dry and to shelter the porch area below. This ridgepole runs east and west and is held 9′ above the loft floor by upright posts (plates 15 and 16).

Putting such a beam in place is always a struggle. Four of us broke our backs trying to lift that huge pole above the 9′ uprights, but even with all that man power it refused to cooperate. After

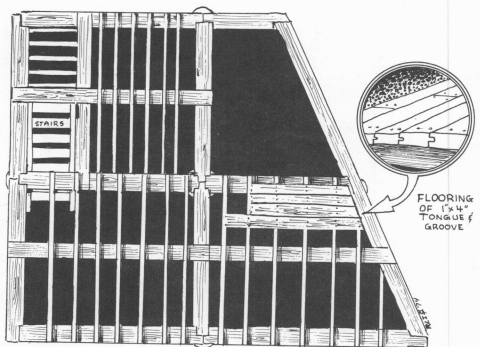

STAIRS

FLOORING OF 1″x 4″ TONGUE & GROOVE

14

several clumsy attempts, we gave up this method of placing it. As I cursed and tried to catch my breath, a welcomed solution came to my mind. I put two 2 x 6 rafters in place, overlapped their top ends and joined them together as a scissor brace. I secured them with diagonal supports and attached a block and tackle to their crossing peak. Then with the aid of my helpers, I hoisted one end of the beam up. I was able to hold what they gained by lifting, while they set up another pair of rafters and raised the other end of the ridgepole in place at the peak (plate 17). Both ends were then spiked to the crossing rafters, and the three supporting uprights were notched into the underside of the ridgepole. The overhanging sections that protruded past the walls were then braced by diagonal poles which were notched into the ridgepole ends and the uprights.

15

16

17

After that mighty beam was put in place, I framed in a 5'-high pony wall on the north side of the roof directly over that wall. On half of the south side, above the floored loft area, another 5' pony wall was framed in. The other half of that side was left open and the rafters for that section were notched in place over the south wall beam. They spanned from 2" beyond that top beam to over the ridgepole and were spaced at 16" on-center (plate 17).

The rafters were spaced at 16" on-center to efficiently carry the heavy 4'-snow load that sometimes collects on the roofs in this area throughout the long winter. This design enables these 2 x 6 rafters to support between 150-175 pounds-per-square-foot, which I hope is more than they will ever have to carry.

The rafter bottoms were noticed over the pony walls and the top wall beams in the conventional manner. A wedge-shaped, double-mitered piece was sawn out of each rafter bottom, and the rafter was then spiked onto the top plate. To figure out the various angle cuts, since I was doing all the cutting with a hand saw (we did not have electricity), I used a sliding "T"-bevel. It is a square that can be adjusted to any angle. I figured out the angles on the first set of rafters by trial and error and put those rafters in place. I loosened the thumbscrew which holds the adjustable bevel blade and pushed the tool in the intersecting corner of the top plate and rafter with the body on the top plate and the blade snug against the angling rafter. I then locked the blade in

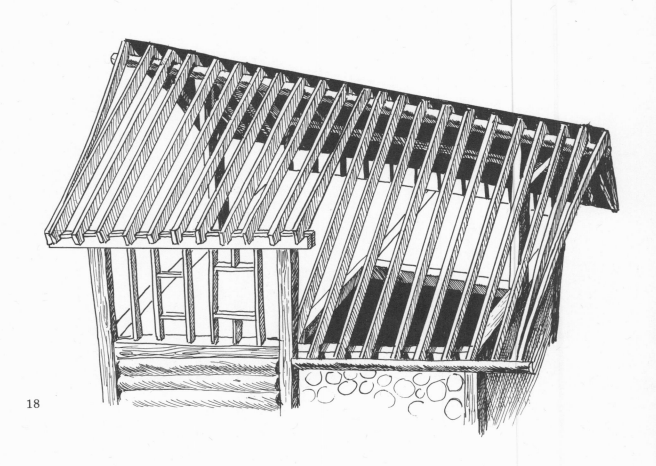

18

place by tightening the thumbscrew and transferred this angle pattern to the next rafter (plate 19).

I cut each rafter bottom end so it was vertical. This was partially a decorative effect, but also a way to prolong the life of the rafters. This cut gives the rafter end more exposed surface, so it remains drier and slows the rotting process. To make the rafter ends have even longer life, I also cut off the bottom point which would collect all the moisture (plate 20).

By the time it came to sheathing the roof, I was exhausted from the past months of steady sun-up to sun-down physical labor. Some old friends from the city dropped by, saw my condition, and volunteered to relieve me of the chore. Within a few hours, all the 1 x 12 boards were up and the house was ready for the finish roofing of 90-weight asphalt building paper. For the next few days I expressed my gratitude the best I could by showing my friends around the beautiful valley.

The rolled asphalt went on very fast. As soon as the roof was finished and the house was protected from the fall rains, we brought the tent and cook stove inside and moved into our new home.

Next came the walls. It was time to figure out what materials we were going to use to fill in between the posts and beams. We wanted to have variety in the walls and wanted to design each a different way. I cut down some standing dead tamaracks which were bone dry from age and filled in the west wall with log pieces while Kathrina framed in the north and east walls. Since whatever materials we filled the walls with did not have to support any structural weight, I used pieces rather than full logs so I could position and frame the windows as I built the walls. I took time to carefully plan the window placement. I set each window up on saw horses and stood back to see the effects

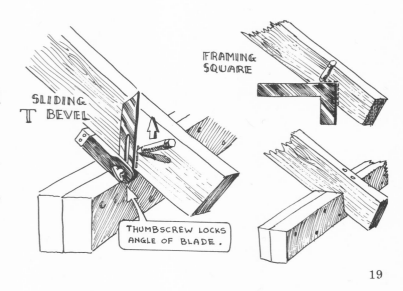

19

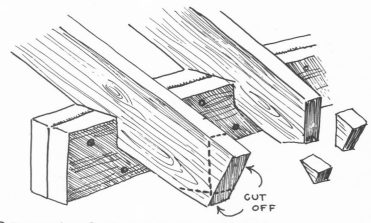

TRIMMING RAFTER ENDS

20

21

22

of every placement. Then when I was finally satisfied, I framed it in and went on to the next. We wanted a lot of window space on this wall because it faces the nearby river. The windows would give us a fantastic view of its relaxing waters while we are at the dining table or in the kitchen (plates 21 and 22).

Since it was canning season already, Kathrina worked several hours a day both canning and framing. She framed in the north wall with 2 x 4's at 16" centers. She built the frames on the floor, then put them in place between the posts and spiked them in. The outside 1 x 12 cedar sheathing was nailed on with galvanized nails to prevent board rot around the nail holes. Galvanized nails do not oxidize as regular nails do. 3½" insulation was then put in between the studs and a layer of black paper covered it as a vapour barrier. The inside cedar sheathing was nailed on later. This wall does not have any doors or windows because it is the coldest wall and does not get any winter sun. The fireplace and staircase are located along it on the inside and a wood shed protects it on the outside (plates 23 and 24).

Kathrina built the east wall in the same manner. Here she framed a large 5 x 5 window which gives us a view of the small, open area that we landscaped and the forest surrounding it. It brings in the morning sunlight to brighten up the long livingroom area (plate 25).

The southern wall has two parts. The section west of the middle post is a log wall made of aged white pine and tamarack. These logs were light in weight and bone dry when I cut them, but were extremely hard to peel, even with a drawknife. These short logs span between the middle post and the long 18" x 72" window to the far west. This long window helps to distribute heat. The cold air comes off the bottom and rolls the heat from the nearby wood heater to circulate

23

24

25

26

27

it through the room. This oblique corner, with both of its long windows in a nice space to relax and read in. It feels separate from the rest of the room and puts someone more in touch with the outdoors (see plate 21).

And now we come to the experiment that failed, the eastern position of the south wall. Here we have a cordwood wall made of bone dry cedar rounds which sat in the house for 6 weeks in 100 degree weather. Even though they were aged and dried they still managed to check and crack within their cement frame. I took extreme care every step of the way to make this wall. I even dry mixed the 1-part lime, 2-part Portland cement, 3-part sand mixture before adding water, to keep it from shrinking. But the cement still shrunk. Even with every precaution exercised, before long the cedar rounds were loose in the cement.

This wall took forever to make. I could only go 18″ at a time because so much mortar was needed between each round. Then I had to wait for that portion to dry before going on to the next. The wall is pleasing to look at, but it doesn't have any insulative value because concrete does not hold in heat. When I look at the wall now I say to myself, there is a month's worth of firewood that we could later use.

This cordwood wall has a window and a door. The window's frame was set into the mortar and seems to be solid in it. The door frame was built as a box and was also set into the mortar. Its sides and bottom are full dimension 2 x 10 bridge timbers and its top is a curved jack-pine nurse log which extends beyond either side to grip the concrete. The door is double 2 x 6 tongue-and-groove cedar. It has no strap hinges and is held together with headless 4″ nails, which were driven in diagonally along the seams between the boards. It has proven to be a good, solid door (plates 26 and 27).

After the walls were filled in, we traded the temporary ladder to the loft for a stairway which begins near the middle of the north wall and goes up over the fireplace. Because of a lack of space, the stariway was laid out to be as steep as possible and not be awkward. Its total run is about 5' for the 8' rise. I wanted each riser to be 9" and the stair treads to be 8" by 30". I mathematically figured out the cuts for the stringers so they could fit accordingly (*see* plate 23).

The roof section is closed in by the loft floor except at its smallest quarter. There, a high ceiling comes up from the livingroom to join the upper and lower spaces and make them as one continuous space which is not closed off by any full partitions. It gives half the livingroom a Cathedral ceiling effect and brings light down to it from the high window of the east gable. This gable, as is the west one, is framed with 2 x 4's and sheathed with cedar 1 x 12 (plate 28).

The loft area has three sections that are defined by rectangular areas. The first section, coming up from the stairway, is our daughter's sleep and play area. It has high railings and is safe for her to amuse herself in. The area directly behind her's is a small storage space. There is a partition between that space and the next. Beyond the partition and the curtained doorway is our 10 x 12 bedroom. It has two low windows at the south wall which bring in light throughout the day and one low window at the west wall which overlooks the river. These windows are at a height that we can look out from while we are lying on our bed (plate 29).

We found that a good way to bring extra heat into a small loft area is to have the stove pipe come up through it. You'd be surprised how much heat is radiated throughout our little bedroom from just that stack (plate 30).

As an afterthought, I dug a 6 x 10 hole,

28

29

30

6' deep, under the back porch for a root cellar. The sides come up another 1' under the porch, making the cellar 7' deep. These short sides that come above ground are insulated with the fiberglas we had left over from the roof. This little cellar has bins on one side, shelves on the other, and a walkway in the center. There are 3 bins, each 2½' deep. They separately store the carrots, beets, and potatoes so their flavors won't mix. The carrots and beets are buried in sand so they will keep better. The shelves on the other wall provide enough space to hold 200 jars, but we never have more than 100 jars to put on them so we also use them as a wine rack. Though we have not yet installed the proper vents, this root cellar maintains about a 46-degree temperature and stays dry. It is a very satisfactory storage space, but if I had it to do over again, I would build it directly under the kitchen floor and have an inside trap door so we don't have to go outside in the cold winter to get our supplies for it (plate 31).

31

It also took away a need or a pressure that had always been hanging on me. This pressure was not relieved when I bought that other house. I never felt I belonged in that place because no matter what I did to it, it would never be an extension of me. It would always be someone else's "trip"; someone else's home.

Though much of my designing in the house was oriented toward saving money, I was definitely not into cutting corners on any of the structural materials. In fact, much of the house was overbuilt. It was designed to be functional, though Kathrina was more interested in how things looked. The planning process was actually a push-and-pull between form and function. It was sometimes difficult to find a balance, but I think on the whole we did very well except for a couple of mistakes—the cord wood wall and the separate crossing beams (plates 32-37).

As I said before, I never really had a home, not even as a child. Because of this I was sparing no energy in building my home the way I wanted it. It was something I really needed to do. When it was done the experience also built something in me. It gave me a sort of confidence in myself and other people.

33

Birch

34

35

36

32

INWOOD '74

DOING WHAT COMES NATURALLY

3

When I was a young boy my father once bought me a Lincoln Log kit. That set of miniature logs captured my interest for hours at a time. Between chores I would sit in the front yard and explore the many building possibilities the kit had to offer. One day when I was pulling firewood out of the bush with our old horse I got an idea to use real logs, modeled from the Lincoln Logs, to make a larger fort; a fort which I could use as a hideout when I wanted to go off alone into the woods.

That fort had everything the smaller set had—only bigger. Even the window and door frames interlocked. But the only problem with my bigger fort was that it was too hard to disassemble and rebuild elsewhere when my hideout was discovered, so I had to construct another one every time this happened.

Designing log forts got to be my primary interest. Whenever I wasn't doing school work or chores I was designing and constructing new forts and figuring out new methods of skidding logs to my sites. I even figured out new ways of bringing in the firewood because I was tired of harnessing the old horse and having to hook him up to logs so he could pull them to our woodshed. It wasn't his fault though—he was a nice old horse. I was just bored with doing that same chore every day.

I devised a pulley system, using an overshot water wheel to skid the logs to the desired sight (plate 1). I really consider myself fortunate to have grown up in a natural environment where I could learn how to take care of my own needs by utilizing its readily available materials. I quickly learned to appreciate the woods. I still use whole timbers in my construction to make use of most of the tree and to escape from having to buy expensive lumber and insulation materials. I admit, building with timbers is a painstaking and sometimes tedious process, but it beats working long hours at a job to save enough money to purchase prefabricated materials. Also I get a certain fulfilling pleasure from shaping each timber and making it fit snugly into place over the others. Each tree that was used was selectively thinned out from my own land and very little was wasted.

My wife and I live on an old homestead which had some poorly maintained buildings on it. They were usable until we could replace them with structures more suitable to our needs. Our homestead has an abundance of gravity water which rushes down from a large creek, irrigating our fields and providing us with our own generated electricity which is enough to power our lights and a few smaller appliances. It has plenty of timbers for construction and heating purposes and has excellent soil for our garden and hay crops. It is also isolated from neighbors and far enough away from town to be free of noise and air pollution. Since it is just what we've been looking for we plan to stay on it for a long time, and we are thoughtfully developing it into exactly what we want.

Our first building project was to replace an old root cellar which had rotted with age. We find it very important to have adequate food storage separate from the house because of possibility of fire. A root cellar also provides a constant cool temperature which keeps fresh fruits and vegetables very well.

The cellar was replaced with tamarack logs. The inner and outer walls were 4' apart and filled with planer shavings for added insulation. Its roof was constructed gambrel style to allow for storage of empty jars, boxes, and other odds and ends (plate 2).

This smaller structure got us back in the practice of building and readied us for the next project, the house.

We chose the site for the house on a slope which overlooks the tallest mountains in the area. This slope is part of a plateau in the center of our land. One one side of it are the hay fields, to the rear was the new barn site, the old barn, and the garden area. In front of the site was a terraced area which we later developed into a tree reserve where we've been pruning evergreens so they grow as full as possible.

We began cutting the tamarack logs for the house in late winter. Most of them came from the mountainside across the field. After they were cut, we left them in place and peeled them with a square-nose shovel before all the sap was up. Peeling them before much of the spring sap flows helps keep them from mildewing and discoloring so readily. The logs remained on the hillside until the snow thawed enough for the horses to skid them to the building sight. The logs were placed there on pole skids and were left to dry for a couple more months.

We mainly used tamarack logs because they have little taper and are usually very straight. These timbers have few limb

knots and are quite durable (plate 3).

While the logs dried, we measured off a 28'-by-30' area and outlined our foundation. The logs were 32'-by-34' in length to allow for at least a 1' overhang on each side. We did not make any attempt to level the slope. Instead, we built our foundation with steps gradually going down the slope. The steps of this stabilizing wall went down at almost two log intervals, allowing the adjoining logs to interlock with the flat rock and cement foundation for added structural support. Each of these adjoining logs was grooved at the bottom so it fit snugly to the log beneath. They were trimmed on the underside instead of the overside to prevent moisture from collecting in the grooves (plate 4).

One of the reasons for the combination of rock-mortar and log foundation was that rock-mortar had to be used where there was contact to ground. The logs would rot quickly if they were touching dampness. Logs, which we didn't have to buy and which were more pleasing to look at, were used where they did not have to be on the ground.

2

INWOOD '74

The slant of the slope provides the house with a 14'-by-30' basement with full headroom. Here, firewood can be stored and a pelton wheel can be kept and protected from freezing. This area also houses an old wood furnace which by gravity heats the upper sections as well as the basement. A cement floor was poured for this area and was slanted slightly downhill for drainage. The surrounding logs are interlocked with round notches as are the wall logs above. A long car axle was driven into these logs at each side to reinforce them where they join the rock and mortar.

The stabilizing walls on the 28' sides were 5" higher than those on the 30' sides to compensate for the stagger of the wall logs. They were constructed 5" higher because 5" is half the diameter of the 10" logs which were used as the end logs.

The longer sill logs rested on the lower wall sections, and the end logs, which would be notched into these sills, would be raised by the higher wall so they could properly interlock with the sills and begin the necessary stagger. Anchor bolts, 12' apart, were sunk into the concrete for added support of the bottom logs (plate 5).

We spaced the joists 2' on-center and notched them into the sills with a lap joint. The joists were left round on the sides and bottom. Their tops were sized and hewed with a foot adze and a broad axe to provide a level surface for the rough-cut 1" subflooring. Before I adzed the joints I made vertical cuts into them every few inches with a very sharp axe (plate 6). It

4

BASEMENT

CAR AXLE

INWOOD '74

5

Raised portion equals ½ of the diameter of the bottom log

6

scoring a log

chalk line

hewing with a broad hatchet

is important to keep your axe very sharp at all times. Then I chopped out the pieces with a 9-pound-head broad axe and went over the cuts with a foot adze to finish them (plate 7). If used correctly a sharp foot adze will make a hewn surface look as if it had been planed by a mill (plate 8).

We set up stringers or uprights every 6' as supports under the joists where needed. Their lengths depended on the sloping of the hill. Their tops were notched and spiked into the spanning joists and their bottoms rested on large rock pillars.

We chose to notch all our corners with round notches because we've found from past experience that this notch looks best and lasts the longest. It allows the wall log to extend beyond the corners, making the notches both beautiful and strong. Our log ends are staggered, one long, one short, so the long one completely covers the shorter one, preventing moisture from collecting on it (plate 9).

I've torn many an old log building apart, and in most cases where dovetail notching was used, the corners were the first place to rot because they were not protected by any overhang.

In my opinion, the round notch is also the easiest of the notches to make. I started my walls by placing the first end log across the two sills, making sure there was an equal distance of overhang on either side. It was secured in place with log dogs. I then took a plumb bob and centered it on the highest point of the log end to line up the new log over the ones below. If you do not have a plumb, any pointed weight, like a fishing sinker for instance, would do just as well. I used this method to keep my walls straight.

To keep the wall logs uniform, I placed any oval or unround log with the widest part going up and down so it could later be hewn to prevent obvious gain. I then used a pair of dividers to measure the gap

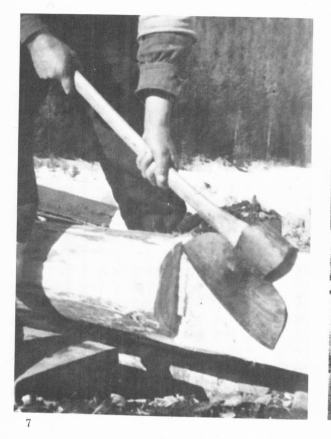

7

8

9

Lap Joint notching
Floor Joists into
Sill Log

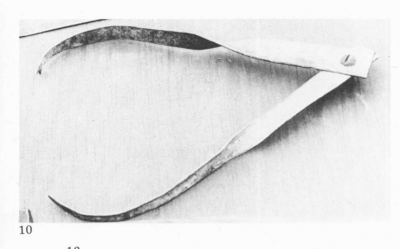

10

between the stabilizing wall log below and the log which was to be notched (plate 10). This gap would be equal to the depth of the notch prior to hewing. The dividers were opened to this size and were held vertical at all times as they were run along the contour of the crossing sill log's end. The upper point duplicated the sill log's contour onto the above log, a gap's width higher than the lower span. The outline of the notch was then marked on both sides of the upper log with a thick lumber crayon (plate 11).

The log was turned over with a peevee and again dogged into place. Then with a very sharp double-bitted axe the notches were scooped out to just beyond the crayon's outline to allow for hewing. The double-bitted axe I've been using was modified for this process, I heated the blades in a vise and slowly bent them to curve them. I then ground off the ends of the blades to round them off so they wouldn't gouge into the sides of the notches as they were cutting them out (plates 12 and 13).

12

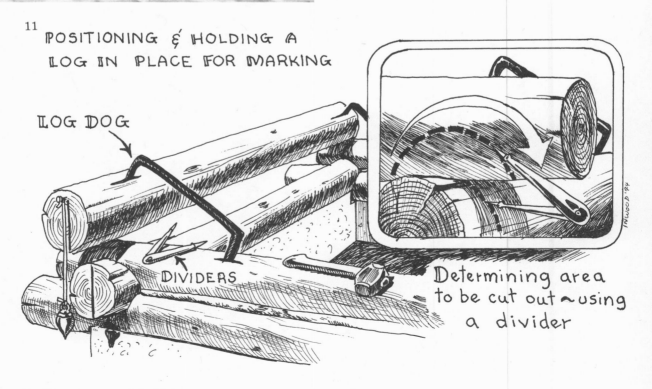

11 POSITIONING & HOLDING A LOG IN PLACE FOR MARKING

LOG DOG

DIVIDERS

Determining area to be cut out ~ using a divider

I learned many times over that it never pays to lift heavy logs in place without the aid of some animal or some simple machine. Too many people cause their bodies needless strain by trying to lift objects which are too heavy for them. Why chance wrecking your back, when with just a little thought and research you can invent a tool to do your lifting? For this purpose, I devised a swinging boom setup that is based on the principle of the log derrick which at one time was used by professional loggers.

I first set up a long vertical pole called a stiff leg because it remains stationary. It could be supported by either a tripod brace or stiff guy fastened to either a floor joist or a nearby solid structure. At the top of this pole, a block-and-tackle is connected to control a suspended, double-poled, swinging boom. At the bottom end, these boom poles straddle the stiff leg and are held in place by a block of wood and a cable. This boom is free to swing around from the bottom and is able to lower logs onto any of the walls. A hand winch was bolted to the bottom of this boom and a pulley was attached to the top of it. The winch's cable went over the pulley and was attached to a pair of log tongs which grasped the center of the log, raising it and lowering it to the desired position. I find this devise invaluable in my work (plates 14 and 15).

The walls of the house went up relatively fast, mainly because many of the logs I used were straight and had little taper. Many of them needed little more hewing than the 3"-flat surface on top and bottom. These logs could be hewn easily enough by marking them with a scribe and scoring them with an axe or a chainsaw, then chopping out the scored section with a foot adze. I made the scribe out of old scrap metal which I found in the dump and I ground the marking tips out of old cobalt steel files. The tips were then

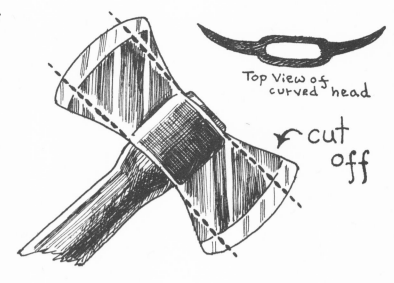

Top View of curved head

cut off

13

14

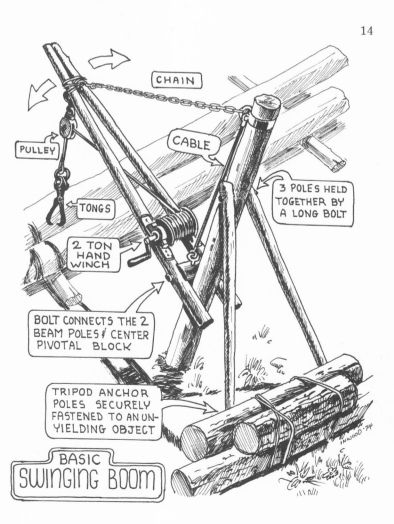

CHAIN

PULLEY

CABLE

TONGS

3 POLES HELD TOGETHER BY A LONG BOLT

2 TON HAND WINCH

BOLT CONNECTS THE 2 BEAM POLES & CENTER PIVOTAL BLOCK

TRIPOD ANCHOR POLES SECURELY FASTENED TO AN UN-YIELDING OBJECT

BASIC SWINGING BOOM

welded onto the metal. One set of these tips is held shut with a piece of wire and the other can be adjusted to various gaps by a block of wood (plates 16 and 17).

Some of the logs were very difficult to fit in places and had to be turned several times before they were straight enough to lay flat over the logs beneath them. These logs either had large tapers or serious bends in them. You'd be surprised how much a log can be corrected by hewing.

There are many purposes for hewing the tops and bottoms of the wall logs. One is to provide a shelf that insulation could be compressed into so it won't be exposed to the weather. I used a mixture of cotton and jute between the wall logs of the house. These materials were the stuffings of a couple old mattresses we had laying around and a davenport I found at the dump. When I ripped open the old davenport with my knife, people at the dump were giving me strange looks. I'd be interested in knowing what they thought I was looking for.

Since the house, I've been using fiberglas insulation. I take a few rolls of the fiberglas and cut through each of them with a saw to get 3″ strips. It is much easier to cut these strips while the wrapper is still on the roll, rather than stretching it out and cutting from long lengths of it. To use it, I just lay out a 3″

The Principle of the Chinese Windlass

15

strip and staple it to the top of a log which has been placed and hewn. It compacts very nicely between the logs and insulates extremely well (plate 18).

Another advantage of hewing the tops and bottoms of the wall logs, or any log for that matter, is to precaution against random checking or cracking. Logs have a tendency to split where the sap wood dries out the quickest or where the sap wood is worked off. Some species, such as young 12″-wide cedar, have as much as 2″ of sap wood all around them. If the log is left round or is hewn evenly on all sides, it will check the heaviest on the side exposed to either heat from indoor sources or heat from the sun, whichever is greater. If the sap wood is cut away from one or two sides the larger checks will develop in those areas. If the logs were hewn on the tops and bottoms, the checking would be hidden between the logs (plate 19).

Another advantage of hewing the tops and bottoms of the logs is a primary interest to anyone who considers his log building a work of art and he wants to appreciate for many years to come. Every log, no matter how uniform it may appear, has some taper and some bend to it. Unfortunately, most logs have a noticeable taper and some high spots which prevent it from seating snugly on

16

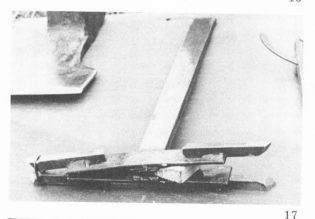

17

Create long strips by sawing thru the coiled roll...

FIBREGLASS FILLS CHANNEL

18

In Harmony with Nature   59

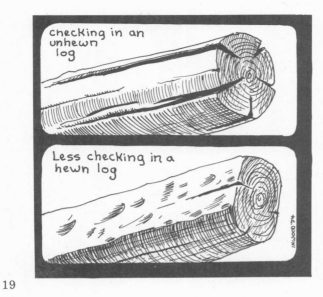

checking in an unhewn log

Less checking in a hewn log

19

20

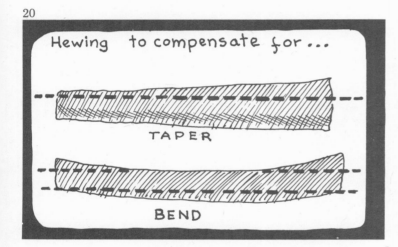

Hewing to compensate for...

TAPER

BEND

21

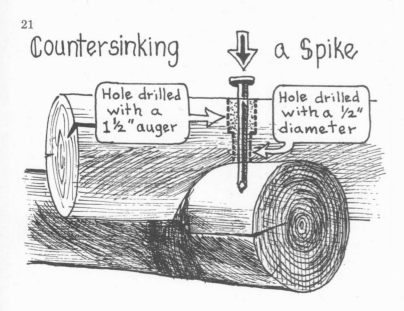

Countersinking a Spike

Hole drilled with a 1½" auger

Hole drilled with a ½" diameter

the log underneath it. To compensate for taper you must hew the gain accordingly. If a wall log as a 9″ tip and an 11″ butt you should hew both top and bottom in such a manner that you gradually cut off an inch more on each side at the butt than you do at the tip. When dealing with a crooked or bowed log, you put the crook or bow up and down and hew the high points until the log is snugly seated. This sometimes takes many turns and much handling before the log cooperates (plate 20).

It is also important to stagger your logs butt, tip, butt, tip to prevent having to hew off larger portions to compensate for gain. This method makes most use of each log.

A common mistake that occurs in most log walls which can also be corrected by hewing is "mouse holes". These are spaces caused by notching too deeply. They should be corrected because moisture tends to collect in them and promote rot in these places.

Each wall was made up of full logs, 32′ or 34′ in length, no pieces. After each log was notched and fitted in place, a 1″ auger hole was drilled half way through it on either side of the proposed door and window openings. A smaller diameter hole was then drilled below the 2″ auger hole to start the 12″ spiral spikes which would be countersunk with a drift punch and mallet to secure the logs together. It is important to spike any future opening from log-to-log to prevent the loose wall ends from collapsing when you chainsaw the doorways and windows (plate 21).

The only disadvantage of using full logs seems to be my wife's complaints of working so long and still not knowing what the inside of our house was like. Upon completion of the walls, I immediately chainsawed a doorway so she could inspect the interior. She was very pleased with the effect of being surrounded by golden tamarack logs and insisted that we find some way to protect them from rot and prevent their losing their color. We did, in fact, coat them with a plastic preservative called Kemwood, which is a brand of urethane. The house has been standing for more than eight years, and the interior looks just as new as it did the day we finished it (plate 22).

After cutting out the first doorway, we tenoned the newly exposed wall ends with an axe and a homemade chisel. The end of the chisel was made from an old car bumper support which I ground sharp on my grinder. The blade part fits into a cut piece of 1″ galvanized pipe. I carved a piece of hardwood to wedge into the pipe for hitting with a mallet (plates 23 and 24). I've used this tool for months at a time without having to sharpen it because of the hardness of the blade.

22

23

A Good Homade Chisel
constructed from...

¾″ galvanized pipe

seasoned hardwood

old car spring steel

filed rounded for gouge shape

pipe

whittle down to fit inside pipe diameter

wood

cut slot to hold tang

cut with hacksaw

slots fit around end of chisel

cut out tang with hacksaw

file or grind desired edge

The ends were tenoned so they could be sandwiched by the double 4 x 4 door frames. Two 2″ holes were then augered into both tenon ends so the log walls could settle independent of the door frame. The double 4 x 4's which I hewed out of logs were placed on either side of the tenoned ends and two smaller holes, large enough for 3/8″ bolts, were drilled into each of them at the bottoms of the 2″ auger holes. The bolts fit through the entire frame and the larger holes allowed the walls to settle without damaging the frames. Pieces of doweling were later fitted over the bolts to conceal them (plate 25).

24

4"x4"

COUNTERSUNK BOLTS

4"x4"

25

Bolt is initially placed at bottom of counter-sunk 2" hole. As the logs..

settle downward, they slide over the bolt; the door frame remains true.

Window spaces were then cut and framed. 4 x 12's, also hand-hewn, were placed vertically against the wall ends and 3 2″-long slots were drilled into each of them. Spikes were then hammered in at the bottoms of these narrow slots. 1″ or so space above, the frame was left open to allow for settling. This space was filled with cotton and jute (mattress and davenport stuffing). When the walls settled, they compressed the insulation and would not damage the windows or window frames. The windows were put in loosely and were held in place with 3/4″ lumber strips (plates 26 and 27).

27

26

Before the top plate logs were placed above the 30' walls several 4"-square laps were notched every 2' on-center into the highest logs of these walls. Ceiling joists which I hewed to a flat 4" top and bottom, were then spanned across from wall-to-wall, and their ends were fitted into the 4" square laps.

The ceiling joists were also supported in the center by a similarly hand-hewn cross beam which spanned across the building to support these beams. The top place logs were then placed over the previous top logs and notched into place (plate 28). 7" cedar rafters were round notched over the top plate logs every 2' on-center above the ceiling joists, except where the dormer was to be fitted in. Here, the shorter rafter pieces were toe nailed to a header above the dormer. To fit the rafters accurately, I used dividers to measure the width of the top plates and cut my notches accordingly. The tops of the rafters were joined together at a final ridge pole which spanned the building at the roof's pitch (plate 29).

We decided that we wanted extra living space in the roof area, so I designed an 8'-by-10' log dormer which has 7' of head room in the center. This area was supposed to be a sewing room for my wife, but it turned out to be a guest room for occasional visitors. To frame the log dormer, 2 x 8 boards were first placed on the already hewn outer-support rafters and were nailed into them. These boards extended from the roof's eaves to where the top dormer side logs would intersect these support rafters. They provided a flat surface for the beveled ends of the cedar side logs. The cedar side logs were round notched to the front dormer logs in the same manner as were the wall logs, and their beveled ends were spiked into the 2 x 8's. Where the top-side logs intersected the support rafters, the bottoms of the valley rafters were nailed in. Their tops met at the ridge pole peak and marked the top-center point of the dormer. At this point the dormer's ridge log was connected to the ridge pole and the valley rafters. It extended horizontally

28

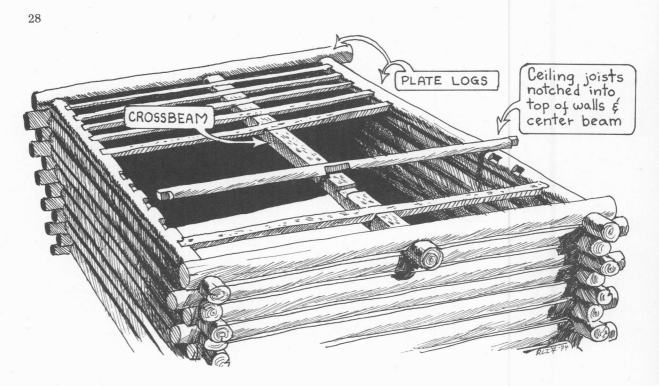

PLATE LOGS

CROSSBEAM

Ceiling joists notched into top of walls & center beam

out to the front of the dormer. Dormer rafters were then round notched to the top cedar side logs and their tops were connected at the dormer ridge. Jack rafters were nailed between the valley rafters and the roof ridge beam for additional support. The front window space was later cut out and framed in the same manner as the wall windows (plates 30 and 31).

After the dormer was finished, the gable ends were closed off with 1″ lumber and later paneled over the cedar shakes. Each gable end has a 16″-square ventilator near the top for air circulation (plate 32). I made nailers for the cedar roof shakes out of smaller poles which I hand hewed with a sharp axe on two sides to a thickness of 2″. Very few of these nailers were straight poles; in fact a lot of them were quite snakey. But even with their bends, hewing them flat on two sides makes them ideal nailers for shake roofing.

I split all the roofing shakes from cedar bolts with a shake froe. The job did not take long and was very satisfying (see chapter 6). After I split these shakes, I took a draw knife and went over them to smooth their surfaces. This I later found was a mistake. Shakes should have a rough surface for proper drainage. The rain water goes into each of the rough crevices and rolls down off the roof. When the shake is smooth, the water tends to penetrate through instead of rolling off, causing leaks in the roof. So much for perfectionism.

The roof eaves are protected from ice buildup by an 18″-wide sheet of aluminum which I nailed to them. The top of the aluminum is covered by the bottom roof shakes to prevent leakage.

With the main structural chores out of the way, it was time to add the finishing touches. We had been collecting rocks for quite a while, in fact whenever we took a vacation we brought back several

29

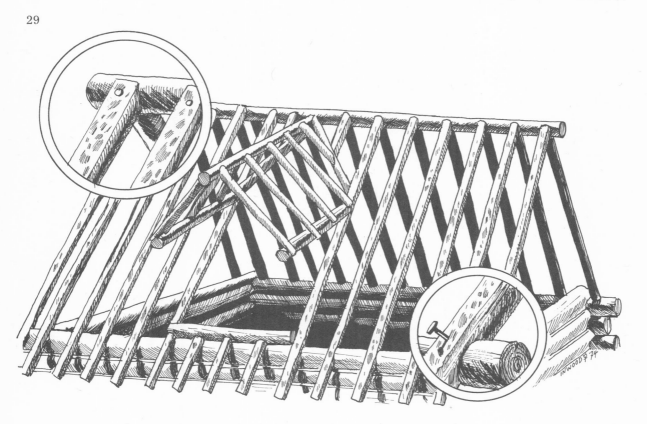

beauties. Our collection consisted of various different types of rocks from Idaho, Washington, Montana, and all parts of western Canada. In my spare time I used to practice splitting the rocks with a rock splitting hammer. I tried to get them as flat as possible for a rock chimney. This chimney is now located at the northern wall, outside the livingroom (plate 32).

A 2'-square hole was cut out of that wall to allow for the chimney pipe of the antique Franklin stove with which we heat our livingroom (plate 33).

Constructing the chimney was very interesting. I first gathered several possible rocks for it and hit them each with a blow of the hammer to check if they easily cracked. The ones that did

were discarded because they were too brittle to work with and too dangerous to use. Such rocks have a tendency of exploding with heat. We bought a commercial flue which has an 8"-by-16" draft opening and began fitting rocks around it. Because it is very difficult to locate the grains in most rocks, I found I had to use the trial and error method of facing them. I had good luck with many of them and was able to split them in half and get two flat faces from one rock. After facing them, I trimmed them so that when in position they would want to tip backward, toward the flue. This way they stayed in place while the mortar was drying. I made other cuts on the end stones to square them off (plate 34).

The mortar I used was a mixture of half

30

JACK RAFTER

VALLEY RAFTER

2"×6"

INWOOD E '74

31

32

33

34

dolomite grit which would fit through a screen that had 200 sections per inch (fine, clean sand works just as well) and half Portland masonry cement. I mixed small amounts, only as much as could be used in a half an hour. Before I mortared the rocks in place, I checked them once more to make sure they would tip inward instead of outward. When I was satisfied with the fit, I added the cement. Whenever there were small openings around the flue after the facing was in place, unshaped rocks were added to fill the gaps. An opening for the settling creosote was allowed at the bottom of the chimney for cleaning. The chimney extends 5′ above the roof for safety (plate 35).

I built forms around the chimney as I mortared the rocks to help it maintain its tapered shape. Each form was a small section, no more than 24″ high to cover the portion which was being worked on. Each was propped up and held in place with poles which spanned from the top of the frame to the ground. The ends of the forms were also nailed to the walls for added support. Later, when the mortar began setting, but before it dried, I removed the forms and swept the excess mortar from the rocks and joints (*see* plate 34).

After completing the chimney, I worked on the interior again. I framed in the room dividers with lumber, built a simple stairway to the basement, and constructed a spiral-type staircase to the upstairs bedrooms. We needed a spiral staircase because of our lack of space. My wife and I agreed that we wanted a large livingroom, diningroom, and kitchen which connected without closing doors. In the space left over, we wanted a good-size bedroom, an ample bathroom, and a staircase. With our design the staircase had to suffer. Its width could only be about 36″, which is convenient

35

for everyday travel but impossible for transporting furniture up and down. All the larger bedroom supplies had to be brought in through the dormer window.

For finishing touches in the house, I designed a dumbwaiter-type wood lift between the basement and the kitchen to send up wood for the cook stove without having to haul it upstairs. The dumbwaiter is a large rectangular box with an open face which has two shelves in it—one for dry kindling to start the fire and one for larger material to keep it going. A small windlass with a hand crank is attached to the framework downstairs to control it. The rope which winds around its drum goes through two pulleys above the shaft and connects to the top of the dumbwaiter. A lever on the windlass' geared handle keeps the dumbwaiter in place until it is to be lowered and restocked (plate 36).

In the kitchen next to the dumbwaiter shaft I designed a kindling cutter which has several notches for different lengths of kindling. The body of it mounts on the wall and the cutter which I made from an old car bumper support and sharpened on the grinder is attached to the top of it. It is free to swing down and chop off

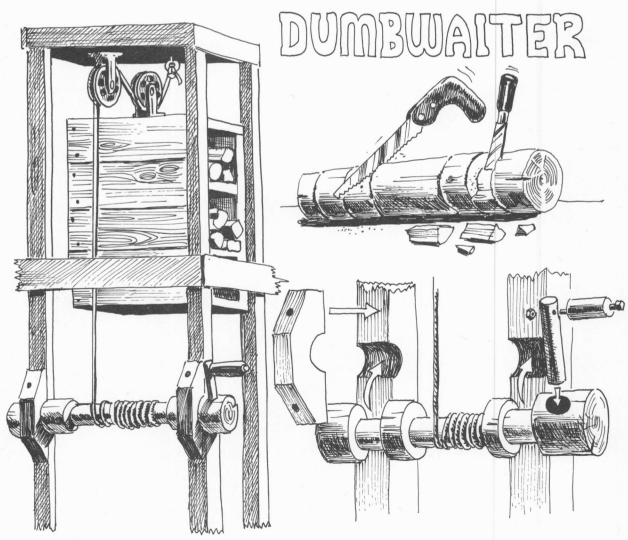

DUMBWAITER

36

pieces with little effort. This device helps keep the kitchen clean by neatly cutting through the blocks without scattering splinters all over the place. It is mounted on the wall so my wife can stand while she is chopping (plate 37).

I also built outside planters out of log. They attach to the front of the house above smaller supports. These logs were dug out with a chainsaw and final cuts were made with an axe to clean them out (plate 38).

My wife and I both stood back and admired the completed house. We were both extremely satisfied with it. The one aspect of the sight we didn't like though was the rocky mound in front of the house. We wanted a proper lawn to accentuate our house's rustic beauty. We found it impossible to grow anything on that rock mound. We were frustrated with that area until the following season when I began plowing the hay field. At

38

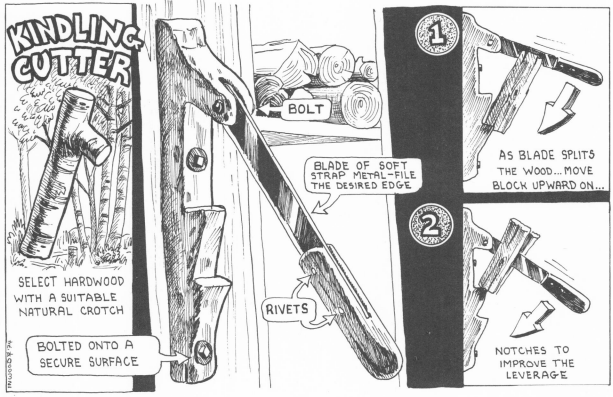

KINDLING CUTTER

SELECT HARDWOOD WITH A SUITABLE NATURAL CROTCH

BOLTED ONTO A SECURE SURFACE

BOLT

BLADE OF SOFT STRAP METAL-FILE THE DESIRED EDGE

RIVETS

1 AS BLADE SPLITS THE WOOD...MOVE BLOCK UPWARD ON...

2 NOTCHES TO IMPROVE THE LEVERAGE

37

that time I had a brainstorm. I carefully lifted large sections of turned furrows and placed them in my pickup truck. I then hauled the grassy mounds to the front of our house and neatly fitted them together like a patchwork quilt. Before long the grass grew out and the sections grew together to make one big lawn for the front of our beautiful home.

The cost of the materials used on the house was very low since I made most everything myself. I spent a long time building it, and my time like everyone else's is valuable, but I can't put any set price on it when I'm doing things for myself. I got pleasure everytimg I cleaned out a notch or put a log into place. I enjoyed it, not only when the notches were finished or when the logs were in place, but also while I worked on them. I don't appear to be a rich man, and I'm not; but I enjoy what I'm doing and I feel good (plates 39 and 40).

39

INWOOD '73

40

4

After completing most of the building on the house and knowing we would have a roof over our heads for the long winter, we decided to give ourselves a much deserved treat. We built a sauna. We have been looking at other people's saunas for several years and incorporated many of their ideas in our own.

Our sauna was built of red cedar logs. Red cedar is a free natural resource in this area. It is light weight and resistant to moisture. It has a wonderful aroma, and of course is a beautiful wood. We used logs because of the excellent insulative quality which is necessary for a good sauna (plate 1).

The inside dimensions are 8' x 8' x 8' high in the center. We have enjoyed saunas in larger and smaller spaces, but we are happy with this size, although sometimes with over five or six people in it, it can feel quite crowded. Of course it depends on what you like. I usually like to stretch out and use up one whole 8' x 2' bench. Our sauna has two of these benches running the length of each side. One is higher than the other, for when we like it hotter.

The logs were peeled several months before and had been set out to dry throughout the summer. We figured they were ready enough to use so we began our foundation. I have seen lots of foundations under log structures; some made out of cement; some out of rock and cement; some with cement or log piers. Some structures had no foundations at all, just logs on the ground. We used rocks for our foundation mainly because they were handy and they are one material we have plenty of. The building site was also a consideration. Our sauna was built on top of a slight hill of porous soil. With a good roof overhang, we would avoid any great water runoff which could move the foundation (plate 2).

To lay the foundation, we dug a trench 6"-deep where the 8' walls were to stand, and set angular rocks into the sand so only their top 6" was above surface. On each corner and midway between two parallel sides, we put in a major-size rock which the sill logs could rest upon. The logs were notched to fit these rocks. Any air spaces between the rocks and the logs were filled with sand (plate 3).

Our next move was to lay the log walls. The cedar logs we used averaged from 8"-to-10"at the butts and from 6"-to-8" at the tips. It was easiest to work with this size because one man could lift and place each log. The wall logs were saddle notched together to a height of 7'. This notch is one of the easiest and it allows for the log ends to extend past the corners (plate 4).

We generally used 12'-long logs to make the 8' x 8' inner square. This allowed at least 1' of extension on either side after notching. Some of the logs near the top were even longer for hanging things on such as towels, clothing, a lantern, etc.

The top plate logs and the center ridge pole are 15' long to support the roof which extends 6′ past the front walls. It covers the dressing porch (plates 5 and 6). A door space 2½′ x 5′ was then chainsawed out above the bottom two front logs.

With the walls up, the next logical step was to set in the floor. I shoveled in and leveled a 4″ layer of sand over the floor surface within the walls, then set in 3″-thick birch rounds with sand packed between them. Though birch is supposed to deteriorate quickly with moisture, the last several months of regular sauna use has not affected the rounds at all. Maybe it was not a good idea to use this wood on sand, but a hardwood birch floor feels good to my feet. If it rots some day, I will probably put in another one of the same material. It's an easy floor to replace (plate 6).

For the sauna roof, split cedar logs were laid, spanning from the ridgepole to 3′ past the top plate logs. The 3′ overhang has proven to effectively shed water and prevent the walls from collecting moisture. The roof has a very small 1′ in 4′ pitch.

1

2

MAJOR ROCKS NOTCHED INTO SILL LOG

SAND

3

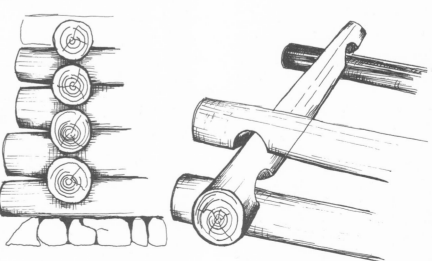

4

In Harmony with Nature   77

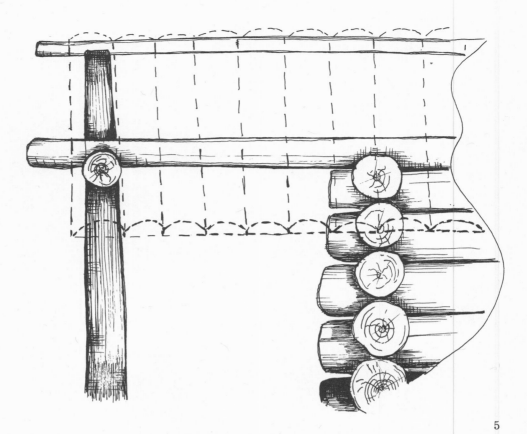

5

By using a subroof of split logs I avoided having to deal with rafters, milled wood stringers, or insulation. The split logs act as rafters as well as roofing. They have an extremely strong insulative quality and are easy to put on. The hard part is ripping them with a chain saw (plate 7).

A vapor barrier of heavy-gauge black plastic was laid over the split logs, then a 4″-thick finish roof of earth was put above the plastic. I threw several handfuls of clover seed on top of it all to hold the sod together. A green grassy covering will soon enhance the beauty of the sauna and help make it fit within its natural surroundings (plate 8).

With the roof completed, the structure only needed finishing touches to turn it into a working sauna. The inside benches and the door were made from 2 x 8 tongue-and-groove cedar. I used this material because I had it, the remains from another building project. I was able to cut the 2′-wide by 8′-long bench boards

in such a way as to wedge them between the log walls, avoiding any need for additional bench supports (plate 9).

The door is like a hatch on a ship in that one has to step over a high floor plate before entering through it. It was built that way for no functional advantages—I just like it (plate 10).

The source of heat in the sauna is wood, of course. We use a small, cylindrical coal stove because it does not take up needed space. The only disadvantage of this stove is that we have to cut our wood in very small pieces. Rocks had been placed on the stove top so that when water is splashed to make steam, the cast iron won't crack.

The stove pipe runs through the wall 3′ above the stove, out past the rear roof overhang, and up 5 more feet so that it extends well above the sod roof. Where the pipe goes through the wall, I cut and framed in a 1′ by 1′ square opening, then packed local, low-fire clay around it to

6

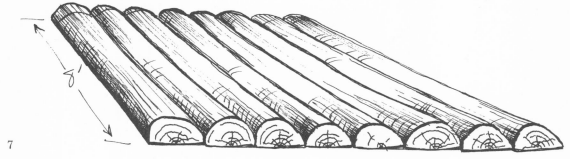

7

8'

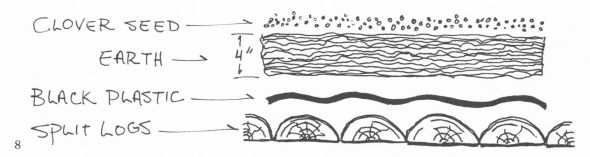

CLOVER SEED $\longrightarrow$

EARTH $\longrightarrow$ $\frac{1}{4}$"

BLACK PLASTIC $\longrightarrow$

SPLIT LOGS $\longrightarrow$

8

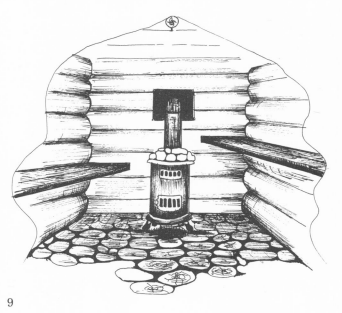

9

10

12

insulate the walls from its heat. As we are using the sauna, the clay is becoming harder. The heat is actually slowly firing it (plates 11 and 12).

One of the last things to be done was to let some light in without losing any of the heat. I drilled holes in some of the logs with a 2½″ auger. In these holes, I set bottles which were the same diameter. Colored bottles do nice things with light. A small, double-paned window was also placed in the door for additional light.

Since the sauna was not near a sizable body of water we bought an old bath tub for the plunge and ran plastic pipe to it. The plunge is a very important part of the whole bathing process. The sauna's heat opens your pores and makes you perspire. This allows the impurities in your body to leave through those open pores as you are relaxing in the hot chamber. The cold creek water which flows into the tub for the plunge rinses off these impurities and quickly closes your pores. It sure stimulates you after a hot meditative sauna.

To light up the sauna you just stoke up the stove, let the wood burn for a few minutes until the chamber is about 180 degrees, then damp the stove down so it holds this temperature. After it's lit, all you have to do is just hop in and let yourself relax and unwind and forget any hassles outside that immediate womblike chamber.

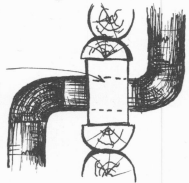

CLAY MIXTURE

STOVE PIPE THROUGH THE WALL

11

5

In the spring of 1969, Shelley and I left our native California in search of land. It didn't really matter where we found it, as long as it satisfied some of the basic criteria we had set for "our place." Being somewhat private people, we knew that the land must be relatively secluded (we had come from 10 acres of country property in California that housed five families and found this type of situation most unsatisfactory for who we are). The land we were looking for must have water, plenty of trees, a low price per acre, and be situated in an area where there is a small community of people we could relate to. We need our territory, as well as we need social contact. We felt lucky to have found a most beautiful valley, some like-minded neighbors and 60 acres of land we could afford.

Our land begins about 300 feet from the highway and then climbs gradually up the mountain through a series of benches. It had been logged 20 years ago and had been able to reproduce a thick second growth of fir, pine, and cedar. Old logging roads intersected at several points on the land, which made immediate travel by car quite easy. It was in one of the logging turn arounds that we decided to build on a very small clearing—at best ¼ of an acre. It is on an upper bench of the land, which would be inaccessible by car in the winter. The spot was quiet, a bit remote, and has a nearby spring from which we could get water.

We soon set up camp in the clearing and

began making lists of priority jobs. A road from the main highway to our bottom property line had to be put in. It just happened that the road was designed to cut through a group of large cedar, fir, and pine trees. As we began the job of felling trees, limbing and peeling them, our original plans of building an "A"-frame house gave way to the obvious and overwhelming urge to utilize these trees in a log cabin. We were pleased that not only were we learning about and actually making a road through the bush, but that the roadway offered us the material for our home.

I can't imagine the number of times Shelley and I sat around the campfire at night, surrounded by a forest we were just getting to know and feel comfortable in and wondering if just the two of us could possibly assemble our home, expand our clearing, bring new life to this area, and claim a portion of territory. Our talk was exciting and exhilarating; our bodies dirty and tired. Each morning we would go out, and after selectively choosing the trees to cut, I would fell them with my chainsaw, then cut a "V" into the top of each of their stumps. This way, I could prop the fallen logs up on the stumps instead of letting them lay on the snow-covered ground until I could get around to skidding them out. I peeled them in that position with either a drawknife or a peeling spud (plate 1). This method worked well and enabled me to do that tedious task without having to bend down to the ground; I just balanced whichever end I was working on up until it was peeled. When I finished that job I left the logs to dry in that position until I needed them (plates 2 and 3).

The logs which had serious bows or bends were set up on skids with their bows up so the weight of the drying log helped straighten itself. Logs should always be peeled no later than a couple of weeks after they are cut. This will ensure clean, easy peeling because the sap under the bark will still be wet.

We needed approximately 40 good-size logs, with an average diameter of 12″ for the walls. We also cut 12 pine poles, 20′ long with 7″-to-8″ butts for floor joists, and 30 small white pine poles, 20′ long with 6″ butts for roof rafters.

Another good reason for raising the peeled logs off the ground was to speed up the drying process and avoid their becoming mildewed from excess moisture. We allowed them to dry on the

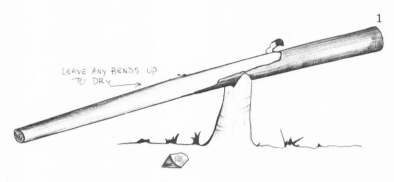

1

LEAVE ANY BENDS UP
TO DRY

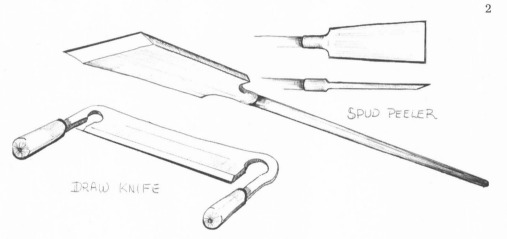

2

SPUD PEELER

DRAW KNIFE

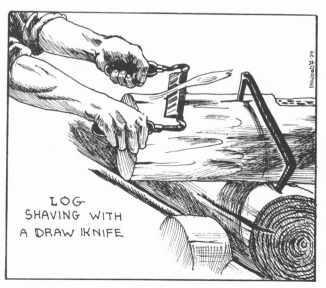

3

LOG SHAVING WITH A DRAW KNIFE

skids and stumps for four months. That summer we searched around for a good house site while we were waiting for our materials to properly age. We thought about the sun and wind and their relationships with the house. We wanted the livingroom to face west so it would get the afternoon sun and the bedroom to be exposed to the morning sun. Because we would be surrounded by windbreaking trees no matter where we picked our sight, we knew wind exposure would not be a problem. We chose to have our house on a bedrock mound at the high end of the clearing. This spot was ideal because bedrock does not shift with the frost. In fact it does not move at all. Nothing can grow on bedrock so we did not have to waste good usable land for our sight.

To locate our foundation piers, we just established a 20' straight line and eyeballed a right angle of 24', then staked both ends and the corner. We repeated this for the other corners and checked to make sure they were square, by first measuring a line 8'-long on one side, and another line 6'-long on its perpendicular. If the diagonal of these points turned out to be 10', the corner would be a true right angle.

After the logs were sufficiently dried we hired a neighbor with a tractor to pull the large wall logs to our site. Logs for the 24' sides were placed in one pile and logs for the 20' sides were placed in another.

We were able to handle the floor joists and the roof rafters with our own pickup truck. With most of the materials at the building site we started the actual construction. There it was, summer already, the hottest time of the year, and we did not even have a foundation set up yet. We really wondered if we were going to have a roof over our heads in time for winter.

The first step of course was the foundation. We used cedar piers, dug 3' into bed rock. We painted them with creosote, then coated the part of the pier to be buried with tar, and wrapped the tarred area in strips of black plastic. The treated piers were set in the foundation holes and packed in the sand. Thirteen of them were spaced throughout the house site (plate 4).

Once these piers were in place, we chose three of our largest logs for the sills. They extended 10' in front of the house as supports for the front porch. They were notched with chainsaw and chisel, then were set lengthwise on the foundation piers, spaced 8' on-center apart from each other (plate 5).

The next move was to notch in the two cross logs at either end of the 24' sills; thus the walls began to rise. We used simple saddle notches on our wall logs because we wanted the log ends to extend past the corners. They are easy notches to make once you learn some of the tricks to them.

The first cross log was rolled into place above the sill log it would be notched to. It was kept from rolling with small pieces of wood acting as wedges (plate 6). It was then determined how deeply this log was to be notched. To measure the notches, divide the diameter of the end of the log being notched in half, and mark that distance on each side of the log exactly where you want the high point of the notch to be. If a log is 14" at the butt and 12" at the tip, the notches will be 7" and 6" deep. Then, with a "T" square mark the width of the under log on the side of the log that is to be notched (plate 7). Remember always to mark both sides of the log and make sure that each tier contains as close to the same size logs as possible, the larger ones at the bottom of the wall and the smaller ones at the top. This ensures that each staggered tier will interlock correctly to the one below it.

4

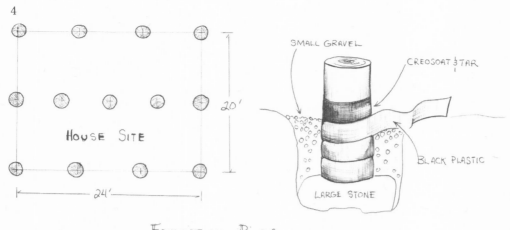

SMALL GRAVEL

CREOSOAT & TAR

BLACK PLASTIC

LARGE STONE

HOUSE SITE

20'

24'

FOUNDATION PIERS

5

SILL LOGS NOTCHED
INTO PIERS

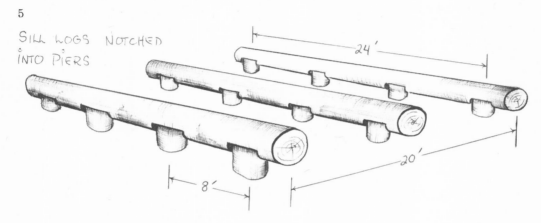

24'

8'

20'

LOGS HELD IN PLACE WITH WEDGES

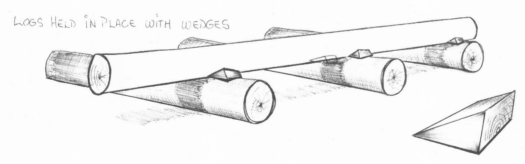

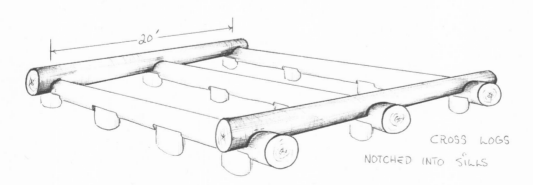

20'

CROSS LOGS
NOTCHED INTO SILLS

6

In Harmony with Nature   85

After you have marked the widths of the under log on the log you are working on, take a scribe, or whatever you can find to estimate with, and mark the contour of your bottom log's end on the upper log. This can be done by eye or with a measuring tape (plate 8).

When the logs have been marked, roll them over so the area to be cut faces up. The logs are held in place again with wedges (plate 9). Vertical cuts, about an inch apart, are then made with the chainsaw. Each cut goes as deep as the lines scribed on both sides of the log end, and with a 1″ chisel and an applewood mallet the pieces are knocked out (plate 10).

When the notch was completed on both ends, the log was rolled in place to be fitted. If the notch needed to be larger, the log was rolled back and more was chiseled out of it. This was usually the case. Sometimes a log was rolled back and forth several times before a proper fit was made.

After the first wall logs were notched over the sills, we put in the floor joists. The sill logs were notched with chainsaw and chisel and the floor joists were set into the sills at intervals of 2′ on-center. They were then spiked to each sill. Any humps or high points in the joists were made level with a foot adze (plate 11). The joist tops were not hewed because we thought it unnecessary to go through all that work just to have a flat surface. A round surface was just as good as long as it was reasonably level. We had to make sure that we butted the ends of the floor boards exactly at the center of the crossing joists to keep everything level.

We used 2 x 6 fir boards for the subfloor. We found that laying an early subfloor gave us a nice surface to work from when we set in the wall logs. It was better than hopping from one joist to another.

With the subfloor laid, we concentrated on the walls. Each wall log was saddle notched in place as described and fitted to the log beneath it. The logs rarely

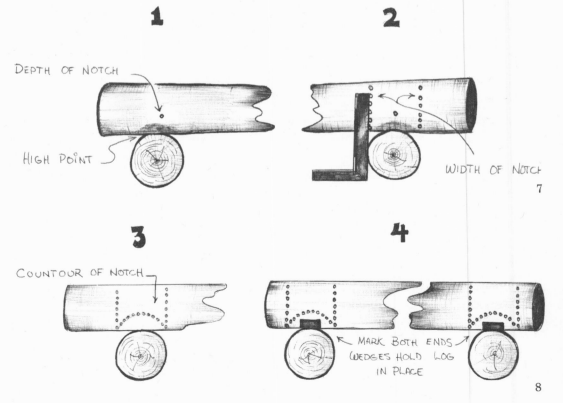

1

DEPTH OF NOTCH

HIGH POINT

2

WIDTH OF NOTCH

7

3

COUNTOUR OF NOTCH

4

MARK BOTH ENDS
WEDGES HOLD LOG
IN PLACE

8

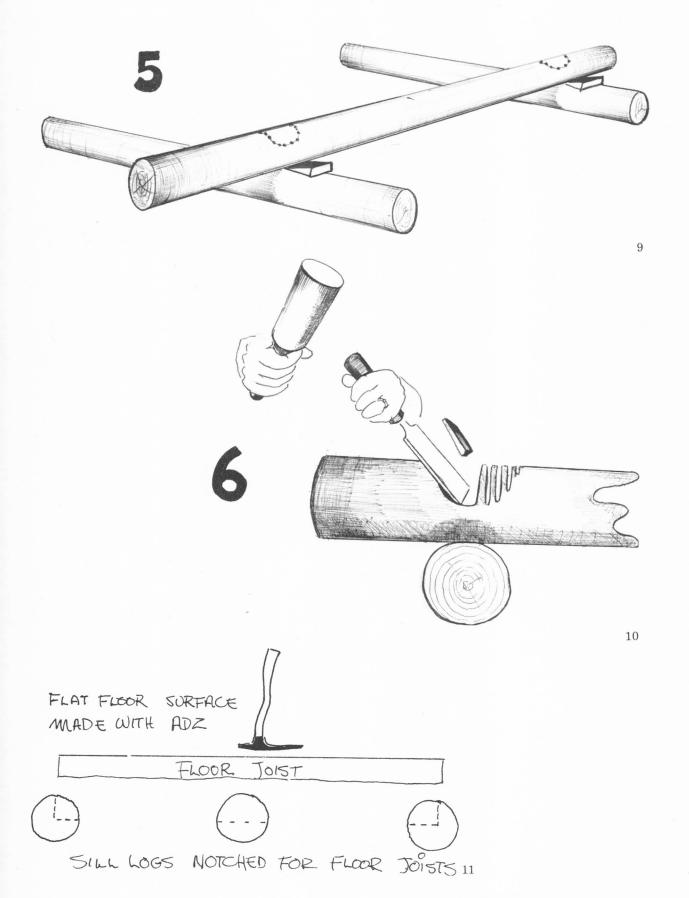

5

9

6

10

FLAT FLOOR SURFACE
MADE WITH ADZ

FLOOR JOIST

SILL LOGS NOTCHED FOR FLOOR JOISTS 11

spanned from end-to-end without having some high points that prevented the two notches from resting snugly on their cross logs. To make them fit correctly, we placed wedges in any large gaps and ran a chainsaw between the horizontal logs. The wedges prevented the top log from settling as the cut was being made. If either of the logs still had high points, we repeated this action until we achieved a tight fit (plates 12 and 13).

We then rolled the top log back and stapled a 2″ strip of fiberglas above the log beneath it. The log was rolled into position one more time and was spiked in place at the ends (plate 14).

Shelley and I could lay eight logs on a good working day when it was not too hot to work. It sure is a good feeling to see your house grow two logs-per-side higher by evening. It gives you something to celebrate about. As our walls grew, we devised a system of using two poles and a rope to roll the logs up from the ground. The poles were used as a ramp, and the ropes, one on each end of the log, were tied to the inside of the building and were run up over the walls. They extended from the ramps, encircled the new log, and were again returned to the inside of the building. We then rolled the new log up the ramp (plate 15). Friends

sometimes stopped by just in time to help us with the heaviest logs, or should I say, we worked on other projects instead of hassling with the "heavies" until friends came by to visit. We raised the walls to a height of 9′, then cut out a door space in the front wall.

The top-side logs and the center beam extend 10′ beyond the front of the building to support a front porch on the upper level, which will be a later addition. This area, since it faces south and gets the full arch of the daily sunlight, will be the site of our small greenhouse. Along with full sunlight, it will also get the heat rising from the house to keep it warm during the winter months.

We set in a vertical center pole and notched it to the center beam above. 20′-long joists were then laid across the front half of the roof to support the loft area. We left the rear 12′ x 20′ section open so it would have a high ceiling and give us a feeling of space.

When we were in Oregon a couple of years ago, we saw an old log barn with a very high peaked roof. That building stuck in my mind because it was so unlike any others I had seen before. I wanted our house to have a roof with a very high peak. I experimented with various-sized upright poles. The higher the uprights,

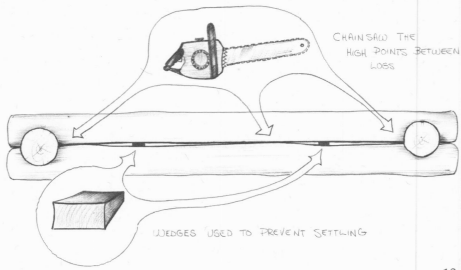

CHAINSAW THE HIGH POINTS BETWEEN LOGS

WEDGES USED TO PREVENT SETTLING

12

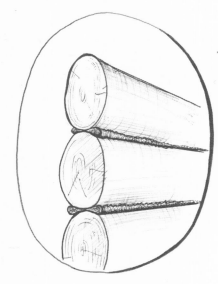

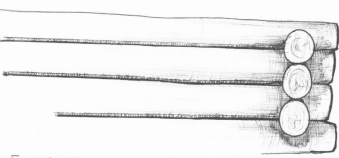

FIBERGLASS INSULATION BETWEEN LOGS

14

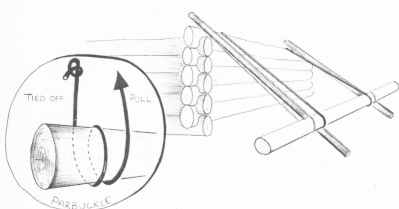

TIED OFF   PULL

PARBUCKLE

15

In Harmony with Nature   89

the more severe the roof pitch. We put up three 16' uprights, one at either end of the center beam and one above the center pole. They were temporarily held up by 2 x 6 braces. I envisioned the roof rafters meeting a ridgepole at the top of those uprights. The peak was incredibly high. I had to wack 2' off the tops of those poles. I peak still seemed too high. I ended up cutting two more feet off the tops, making the uprights 12' in length. A ridgepole was notched in across the tops of the uprights, then the rafters were set in place.

The 22 rafters were spaced at 2' on-center. Each spanned from above the ridgepole to 18" beyond the walls, giving the house long eaves to protect the walls from direct precipitation. The top side logs on each side were notched at right angles where the rafters met them. Each rafter was notched the same way to set into the top logs. They were then spiked into place at those joints (plate 16).

The tops of the rafters extended enough past the ridgepole to cross with the rafter coming from the opposite side wall. Though they were all cut the same size, 19', some were longer than the others when they met the ridgepole. We sawed off the tops of each rafter at an angle so they could face each other where they rested. They were then spiked in place (plates 17, 18, 19).

The next job was to nail on the double roof. 1 x 8 fir boards were used for the inner roof. They were nailed across the rafters and covered with tar paper. 2 x 4 spacers were placed 2' apart above the fir boards. Then came 2½" of fiberglas insulation which fit between the 2 x 4's. The roof was finished with sheets of thin galvanized steel that were nailed to the spacers. We chose this material because it sheds snow well, which means we do not have to climb up on this roof every winter to shovel it off. Galvanized sheeting also reflects heat, keeping the house cooler in summer and warmer in winter. I must admit, it's not the most natural roofing we could have, but it sure does its job well.

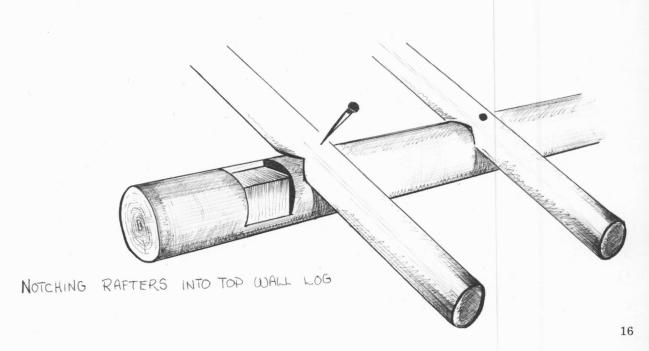

NOTCHING RAFTERS INTO TOP WALL LOG

16

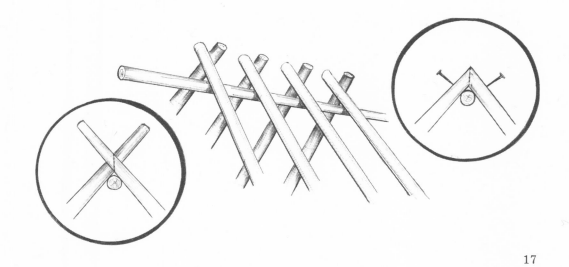

17

18

BASIC POLE
STRUCTURE

The roof has so high a pitch, that we could suspend a clothesline under it, and the clothes hanging from it would be far enough above the main level that they would not be in anyone's way.

The main floor is finished with 1 x 6 hemlock. It radiates out in four triangles from the centerpole and spreads to the ends of the walls. After the floor was laid, we built a staircase to the loft area so we could put in the flooring up there (plates 20 and 21).

The loft area is approximately 10' x 12'. It has a double floor of fir 1x boards. Our bedroom area is located here. At the east wall of this area, we put in a 5'-wide dormer with a peak that extends 7' out past the roof line, directly over the log wall. The morning sun comes in from this small study area to get us up bright and early (plates 22 and 23).

The gable end, south of the loft, has two windows and a door which allow the midday sun to brighten this area. The window that opens was placed directly across from another opening window at the north wall for good cross ventilation. They also release the warm, rising air and aid circulation. The door to the porch terrace is a "Junky John" special. "Junky John" is the local dealer of any used item from toilet bowls to electrical supplies. Sometimes, if the offer is right, he even sells you things from his own house as his wife stands in the background cursing in Russian (plate 24).

The end gables were paneled inside and out with 1 x 8 cedar boards which were nailed to 2 x 4 frames. They were insulated with fiberglas insulation.

One of the main advantages of using full-length logs for the walls instead of pieces is that you do not have to figure out where you want the windows until you have lived in the house awhile. They also make the walls more structurally sound and have a more pleasing aesthetic effect. We definitely wanted several large windows at the west wall so we could get full afternoon sunlight and could see the sun set over the mountains. The kitchen and living areas are facing that wall. From the large windows, we can watch everything grow and fade with the changing seasons in our landscaped clearing and our rock-lined garden (plates 25 and 26).

19

20

21

22

24

23

25

26

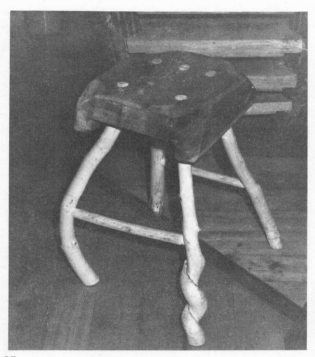

27

Since most of the structural work has long been finished and we are living comfortably in a well insulated, cozy house, we now have more time to enjoy and learn about our surroundings. Already, in some of the places where I cut the logs and thinned out the evergreens, huckleberry and elderberry bushes are sprouting up all over the place. Every once in a while I take time from my daily chores to thin out more areas so other small plants can get the needed sunlight and can feed from the limited nutrients in the soil. I use a lot of the wood I take out for making furniture and other useful objects.

In the past few months, I've made several pieces of furniture that fit in with the rustic style of our house. A couple of my favorite pieces were made for the newest member of our family, who has inspired a great deal of creativity (and other emotions) in both Shelley and I. Using nature's own bent and spiraling designs, I made her a high chair out of vine maple and pine (plate 27). I also made her a crib which interlocks together with the trimmed ends of its own rails fitting into the augered holes of the upright posts (plate 28).

I am learning much about working with wood as a hobby, as a necessity, and hopefully someday, as a source of income. Wood is very satisfying to work with and will always be plentiful if people will learn to be selective about their cutting. If a forest area is thinned out instead of wiped out, the removal of many crowded trees leaving one tree standing in every 10' or so, will actually promote the growth of that area. The trees remaining will be able to grow straight and tall and will receive all the sunlight and nourishment they need. In the years to come, as we are doing now, we will preserve our wood lot and make it a more beautiful area by thinning it out in this manner.

We realize how important wood is for
our future survival and yours (plates 29
and 30).

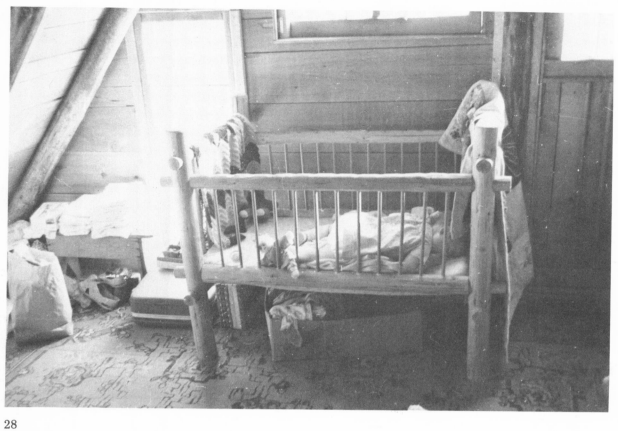

28

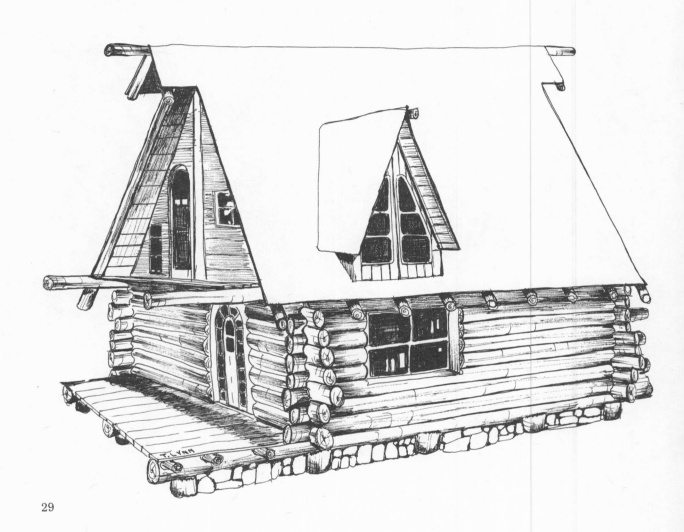

29

30

6

Ye Shall Know Them By Their Works

INWOOD '74

Since my childhood I've had a longing in my heart to go back to nature and once there, to become self-reliant. Like many people, for whatever primitive motive, I wanted to step back into a wooded wilderness with nothing more than a trusty axe (and in these modern times, a chainsaw), a rifle, and just a few other belongings. I wanted to live off the land, build myself a little log cabin, and become one with the natural order of things. But because of immediate necessities and a learned societal craving for financial security, I had to compromise these yearnings and enjoy a creative outlet within the environment I was familiar with—the environment from which I was receiving my "daily bread." This creative outlet was painting. I spent several years in colleges and universities, and at one time had a strong ambition to become a university art instructor. I was among those many qualified potential university instructors who received terminal degrees in art but who were not successful in finding suitable teaching positions because of a wave against the support of higher learning institutions.

So I was left without a job. But because of the order of things, I could begin thinking about those things I have always wanted to do. In effect I was coerced into finding alternative goals and doing the two things I wanted to do most; start my own art school to share some important ideas I had about art and to go out into the woods and hack out an existence for myself and my family. I founded an arts and crafts school and taught at it for 22 months. At that time, the nearby community was too small to support such an endeavor, so I gave it up and devoted my energy to developing our little homestead. In the process I have discovered the importance of working together with my family toward a common goal.

The first few months that we lived on the land seemed like an extended vacation from the former ratrace. We found solace in nature and in hard physical work. We cleared areas and set up a temporary camp. We spent very little money and kept ourselves busy doing what needed to be done. We made rough plans for a wood shed, an out-house and corrals. We picked a building site that was relatively level and decided it was there we wanted the house. We agreed not to employ any heavy equipment on the land. We even park our car near the road to keep from disturbing the natural setting.

Though I had previously worked as a laborer on a couple of ranches and did log work while employed by the U.S. Forest Service, we were somewhat inexperienced and idealistic about our approaches to the new land. I had also made a giant monkey-bar set out of logs for a large playground but I had never built anything like a house. Still, I had a pretty good idea of where to begin from having read many books to learn a few basic techniques and having a memory full of building ideas that went all the way back to my childhood. I wanted to build a house of my own design and imagination without any conventional materials except for nails and a few tools. I knew that with practice I could eventually develop my own building techniques and be satisfied with my achievements.

It didn't take very long for my plans to begin materializing. I soon recalled much of my previous knowledge. I remembered the way the Forest Service used to peel logs for the quick structures they built. They would cut the log to size, and with a sharp ax cut off thin strips of bark on three sides of the log (plate 1). This allowed the moisture to escape from the peeled areas and also controlled checking. The remaining three strips of bark would easily peel off after the logs dried out and shrank. This would take anywhere from one-to-two years. Then when the seasoned logs would get a good soaking from a heavy rain, the bark could be easily removed. This method also produced a nice color effect. As the peeled areas aged, they turned grey. The protected areas stayed a golden-to-rust color until the bark loosened. The log when fully peeled has an incomparable rustic effect.

I found the chainsaw to be my most valuable tool. As I knew from previous experience, nothing could surpass its efficiency and speed in cutting and bucking firewood or felling and limbing trees. While it is a machine and like machines it is sometimes temperamental, with experience you begin to learn what it can do for you. It also costs a bit to maintain, but everytime I rip through logs to make my own boards and cut poles to the size I want, I realize that I could not do these jobs by myself any faster or cheaper with any other tool. However, just as a matter of personal taste, I use the axe for limbing and notching. It may take longer, but there is a certain satisfaction in using an ax and it doesn't cost anything in gasoline and oil.

1

LARGER ROCKS AT THE BOTTOM →

2

3

Since the construction job was primarily my own, and because we could not afford hired help, I had to design a method of building our house in which I could handle all the materials by myself. Though my wife was on the project with me, she was busy with housekeeping chores, gardening, animal maintenance, and civic activities. I didn't want to be calling on her every few minutes to help me fit something in place or assist me with other awkward jobs. The building had to be a one-man effort with light-weight and easy-to-handle materials.

We chose the site for the house on a slight slope overlooking our garden and the pasture on which our two-year-old colt was tethered. I compensated for the slope with fir pillars of varying lengths which were set on stone foundations. Fir was chosen because of its strength, weather resistance, and ability to hold nails.

The pillars were very short at the top of the slope and gradually longer toward the bottom. Each pillar was pealed on three sides, and each rested on a pile of rocks which went roughly 2½' down into the ground. The ground was grainy and porous so it provided adequate drainage. The foundation rocks were larger in the bottom of the hole and gradually got smaller toward the top for added drainage and strength (plate 2).

The rear kitchen and dining room area was built on the same level into the slope. As the terrain dropped away, storage space was provided for under the front unit (plate 3).

The rear section is many sided; it gives us the room we need for cooking, cleaning, and dining. And it lacks the monotony that the traditional four-sided room can have. The original floor plan, comprised of seven floor joists of various lengths, fanning out from a 9' beam in front to a 19′ beam, was located at the far rear into the slope. The distance between the two beams is 12′. These beams were notched over the five vertical posts beneath and they were each hewn level. Even at that point, I could tell that the space wasn't going to be adequate so I added two 10½′ beams which were almost at right angles with the 19′ beam. Another floor joist was added to either side to secure the beams and lengthen the floor support. On the east side of the area, an 8′ beam was notched to the front of the 10½′ beam and was connected to the front beam. On the west side I added two other beams to include space for a doorway and a stairwell. I then added another 2′ area into the slope behind the 19′ beam for seating space, storage, cupboards, and counters.

The 9 x 12 front section was a bit simpler. It was raised on six upright supports. The two uprights in the rear also support the 9′ beam in the kitchen area. Two other uprights are in front of these forming a square. The other two are in front of the others. They border the 3 x 9 closet area. This section was framed with log floor beams, and three joists were added for more support—two running lengthwise on either side of the doorways in the 9 x 9 section and one going across to frame that section (plate 4).

With the pillars and joists in place, it was time to work on the subfloor. I went around to several of the local mills and priced some low-grade 2 x 10's and 2 x 12's, but the cost was beyond my means no matter where I went. So I decided to make my own boards. I first felled a tree. After felling it, I left it where it was.

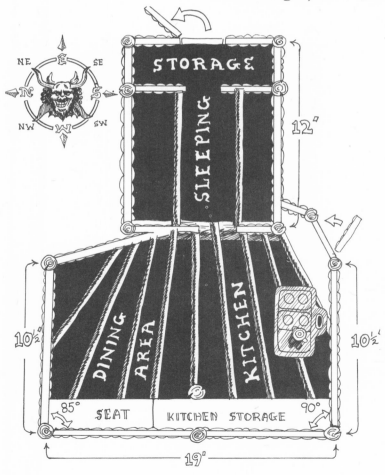

4

Then I limbed off the branches from the butt to the length I wanted the boards to be. The tree was dropped across a stump or blocks, making the butt of the tree stick out parallel above the ground. The lower branches were then trimmed off, and the upper branches were left intact to prevent the tree from rolling while I chainsawed. I stood along the side of the tree, started my chainsaw, and began cutting off one of the outer slabs. I used a downward motion like one would use when bucking cord wood. I didn't use any device for measuring the thickness of the cuts, I just eyeballed them, and before long the boards were coming out reasonably straight (plates 5–10).

After each board was made, it was detached from the log (plates 11 and 12). You wouldn't believe how the first few boards I made looked. They were so warped and their widths varied so much from end-to-end that I really didn't think they could be used, not even for the subfloor. But by doing some hewing I made them usable.

With practise, I developed the technique of ripping my own boards. I learned to keep my chainsaw very sharp and to file the rakers of the chain lower than usual (plate 12A). That enables each tooth to take bigger bites out of the wood. But if the rakers are too low, the chain grabs the wood too much instead of sawing through it.

Most of my boards are about 1½"-to-1½" thick. They are of white pine and cedar because these are softer woods which are easier to cut through. White pines in our area don't have much taper and are very straight. Long boards can be cut from them. They would produce boards which were the same width from end-to-end if my cuts were straight.

Since we live in an area that has cold winters, we wanted to make sure we had a well-insulated floor. We covered the subfloor with a vapour-barrier layer of black building paper and spaced 1½" pine saplings about 16" across the paper. 1¼" boards were then placed over the pine saplings as a temporary finish floor. I later spaced more pine saplings over it, and added a final board (fiber) floor. Needless to say, with all these layers we haven't any problem with cold or dampness coming through the floor (plate 13).

When I was a young boy, growing up in Idaho and Montana, I saw many old lambing and pioneer sheds. They had post-and-beam walls which were sheathed or paneled with rough lumber or vertical slabs. They sure seemed to have been around for a long time. I liked that method of building, so I incorporated it into my house using half rounds for siding. I further modified this style to give the house proper insulation qualities by adding a few more layers of boards in order to add strength and to help keep the heat in.

I set up and nailed in five posts on either side of the front area and a post on either side of the doorways of the 9' sides. Beams were notched and spiked across the tops of these poles to brace them and tie them together. Diagonal poles were then added for more support. The sections without windows had diagonals spanning from the bottom of one corner to the top of the opposite corner. The sections with large windows didn't have any diagonals. The headers and sills of those windows provided horizontal support because they were notched solid into the uprights. The sections in the far front have smaller windows which are also framed into the uprights. There are additional braces below the bottom sills of those windows to make sure the walls won't go anywhere.

The same basic plan was followed for the kitchen-dining area walls. What

5

6

7

8

In Harmony with Nature

9

10

11

12

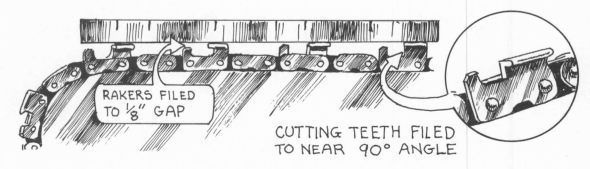

CHAINSAW SHARPENED for RIPPING

RAKERS FILED
TO ⅛" GAP

CUTTING TEETH FILED
TO NEAR 90° ANGLE

differed was the placement of the diagonal bracing. Instead of the braces in sections without windows going from the bottom corner to the opposite top corner, they only went from the bottom corner to the middle of the opposite pole. Though this method was sufficient and used less materials, the method used in the front section was far superior structurally. It could support more tension without giving way, because the diagonals are wedged into opposite corners and were braced by them. The larger windows in the rear section have "V"-braces under them which consist of two poles that meet in the center of the floor beam and span to opposite posts under the bottom window sill (plate 14).

I was now faced with the problems of how to make the walls thick enough so I would not need store-bought insulation and give them a finished look. I came up with the idea of using peeled half rounds. I ripped 6"-to-10" logs, peeled them, and spaced them upright against the outside of the post-and-beam frame, then toe nailed them in place. Small quarter rounds were then ripped and placed between the half rounds to fill in the cracks.

Many 5"-6" diameter cedar saplings were then ripped in half for an inner layer of sheathing. These half rounds were nailed side-by-side, and quarter rounds were later added between them to seal off the walls. This inner wall is

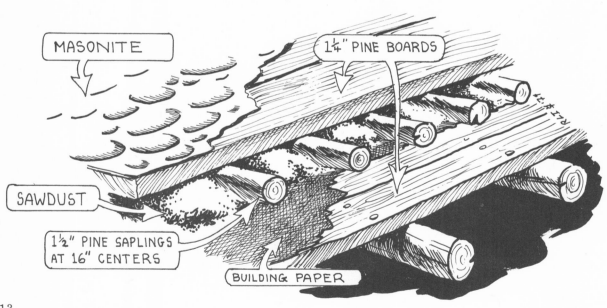

MASONITE

1¼" PINE BOARDS

SAWDUST

1½" PINE SAPLINGS AT 16" CENTERS

BUILDING PAPER

13

both decorative and adds to the insulative qualities.

Each season the quarter rounds can be wedged deeper into the spaces between the half rounds as both layers dry with age. The tighter they are driven in, the greater the wall's ability to seal the dead air spaces between the slabs. When the wall is properly sealed its insulative quality is excellent and does not cost much. To finish off most of the walls, many more poles were ripped and their half rounds were set upright side-by-side along the inside of the post-and-beam frames. They were then nailed to that frame (plate 15).

I made sure to cut the ceiling joists 6′ longer than the end of the walls to allow for 3′ of eave overhang on each side. These joists were then notched into the upper log of the double top plate. They act as floor supports for the loft and prevent the walls and roof from spreading. The longer the eaves, the more the walls are protected from the weather. But to have long eaves, you must make sure to properly brace them because there is a great amount of snow and ice that builds up on this area. I not only extended the ceiling joists to the end of the eaves, I also notched in diagonal braces from the upright posts to the ends of the joists for additional support (plate 16).

Long eaves are a disadvantage when the house they are on is surrounded by a forest. In colder seasons, the long eaves will tend to prevent the warm sunlight from shining on the walls and entering the windows because of their shading effect. But in hot weather this is an advantage.

The end ceiling joists also act as end logs to begin the loft area. The loft is the small area above the piano and children's room

14

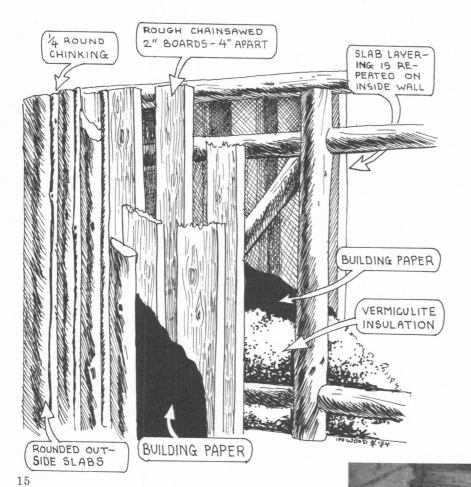

¼ ROUND CHINKING

ROUGH CHAINSAWED 2" BOARDS – 4" APART

SLAB LAYERING IS REPEATED ON INSIDE WALL

BUILDING PAPER

VERMIGULITE INSULATION

ROUNDED OUTSIDE SLABS

BUILDING PAPER

INWOOD '74

15

16

which we use for our sleeping quarters. It is 5' high at the peak and is four logs and a rafter high on either end. The loft gables are made up of three horizontal logs which were round notched to one another and several smaller stockade rounds which follow the roof's slope. At each end there is a window for light and ventilation. They were carefully made large enough for us to crawl through in case of fire (plates 17 and 18).

To make the roof's slope, I simply extended two poles over the gable ends and met them at the peak in the center. This gave the 5' peak. We didn't need a higher space because after all we were just going to sleep in this area. To raise the peak would give us more space to heat and a greater chance of heat loss. We wanted the ends of the loft to be a bit higher, so we raised them by adding a 5" diameter log on either side above the eave supports (*see* plate 16).

A second set of roof rafters was put up at the rear of the loft and a 24' ridgepole was nailed to their joined tops. Two 24' purloins were notched in across the center of the rafters. This framework was then cross braced in many places so it could support the heavy shake roof and an extra heavy snow load (plate 19).

Included in the roof supports is a set of two angle-braces which hold up the 8' front extension (plate 20). Roofs are often the first section of a structure to go. They collect all the weather and have the greatest tendency to rot and weaken, therefore they should be well made.

Instead of laying rafters for the roof, I decided to rip extra thick boards and span them from the ridgepole to the eaves. These boards take the place of rafters and provide the finish roofing with super-strong supporting nailers. These nailers are made of fir because this wood is almost as weather resistant as cedar

17

18

20

19

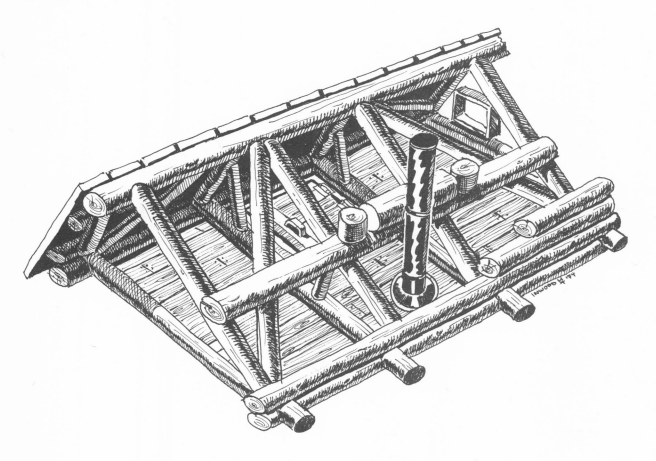

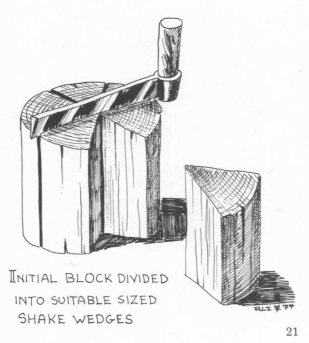

INITIAL BLOCK DIVIDED
INTO SUITABLE SIZED
SHAKE WEDGES

21

22

and is as strong and durable as any of the other evergreens. It also holds nails much better than cedar.

To make your own roof shakes you need several log bolts. Each should be between 18″- and 32″-long, depending on how long you prefer your shakes; it's all a matter of personal taste. I like to use 21″-long shakes because they cover a substantial area and they can be overlapped nicely to prevent leakage. For me this length is easier to make than the usual longer ones because our shake trees are young and small. They have twisted grains and many knots. To find ideal shake material, you should go where a logging company has logged an area rich in first growth cedars. There you will find many high stumps that were left after the slaughter. Such stumps, which are over 18″ in diameter and have at least 6″ of radius before the center rot, are an excellent source of shake bolt material.

To make these shakes, I take a mallet and froe and split the bolt into several sections (plate 21). A section is placed on a stump or log round, then the bark and outer layer of soft sap wood is trimmed off. Half of the top of the working stump or round is cut out to make a safety ledge. The half that remains acts as a back stop to provide better control of the shake sections as they are being worked on (plate 22). The next step is to trim off any portion of heartwood that is dry rotted (plates 23 and 24). With a froe and a hard wood mallet, the shakes are then split off the bolt section. The bolt section should be turned end-for-end each time a shake is split off. This develops the taper effect of the shakes (plates 25–28).

Because of the poor quality of our shake trees, I had to make thick, 1″-to-1½″-wide shakes; but I'm beginning to like heavy shakes. Most homemade or commercial shakes are half that thickness. Heavier shakes are more durable and offer a

23

24

FROE

TURNING BOLT OVER

PRODUCES WEDGE SHAPE

25

26

27

28

superior insulative factor. Shakes are cheap if you make them yourself and they are, to my eye, the most beautiful of all roofing materials.

To lay the shakes on a roof, you start from the eaves and nail down the top ends of a full row of shakes to the accommodating nailer. To do the second row, you start a third of a shake's length up until you complete that whole row, then repeat this procedure. Note that each row covers a large portion of the row below it. This ensures a 100% leak-proof roof (plate 29). This method is continued until the roof is finished. At the top of the pitch, a ridge cap of aluminum or some other material is placed over the highest shakes. It ensures against leakage at the peak of the ridge (plate 30).

My next job was to hang a door. With that the house was sealed off from the weather and was ready for us to move in. This massive door was made out of fir boards on the outside and cedar half-rounds on the inside (plates 31 and 32). Between the two layers is a vapour barrier of building paper and a layer of 1x's spaced a few inches apart to create a dead air space for insulation (plate 33). The door was finished off with a locking bolt on the inside which was secured in place with 8″ lag bolts (plates 34 and 35).

I really enjoyed the interior work that followed. From leftover cedar, and other, half-rounds that I ripped for the purpose, I made cabinet doors (plates 36–39). Using small birches, I designed diningroom chairs (plate 40), and a dinner table (plate 41).

I wanted everything in our house except for stoves and cooking facilities to be hand-made, nothing store-bought. I had little choice in the matter actually, because of our financial situation.

After we had a suitable roof over our heads and a warm living quarters, I started working on other necessary

29

30

31

32

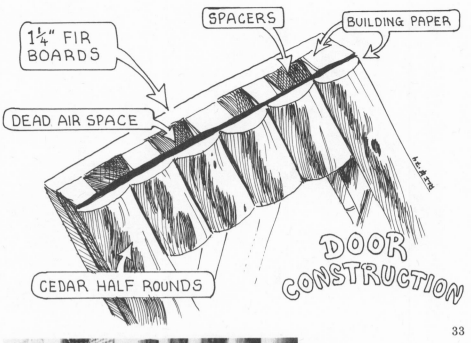

1¼" FIR BOARDS

SPACERS

BUILDING PAPER

DEAD AIR SPACE

CEDAR HALF ROUNDS

DOOR CONSTRUCTION

33

34

YEW TREE

35

36

37

38

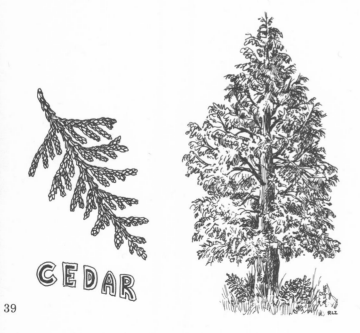

CEDAR

39

40

projects. One such project was to make a bordering fence around the horse's pasture. Because our ground is very rocky and is difficult to dig fence posts into, I built a jack fence instead of the typical post-and-rail fence. To begin this fence I first cut a few hundred poles to length and brought them to the site. I took two short poles, about 6' or 7' in length and notched them together near their tops to create an inverted "V"-jack. These jacks were spaced every 16' or 17' apart to receive the horizontal poles which were notched and joined to them. The legs of the jack prevent the fence from falling forward or backward. A diagonal brace, running from the crotch of one jack to the bottom of the leg of the next jack, was put in at every fifth section of the fence to prevent any part of the whole structure from collapsing lengthwise. They were placed on the opposite side from the horizontal poles so as not to interfere with them. A jack fence also has one line of poles running horizontally at the bottom of the jack legs on the back side of the fence. This prevents the leg of the jack from being accidentally forced sideways, thus undercutting the support. The horizontal poles on the front of the jack are alternated, butt, tip, butt, tip, to balance out the weight on each jack. Also, the jack leg on the uphill side is shorter than the one on the downhill side to maintain balance.

The front of the fence, the side with most of the horizontal poles, should be facing the livestock. This side can withstand the most pressure. Otherwise the poles are subject to being forced off the jacks when the fence is rammed by a frisky animal (plate 42). This design of course is reversed when used to contain goats or sheep because these nimble creatures are apt to climb the progression of horizontal poles (plate 43).

Perhaps something should also be said

about my well. I dug a 10'-deep hole, below the water level, down to a bedrock base. This hole is 6' in diameter and is lined with a hefty boulder cribbing which encircles the well opening. The boulders for this cribbing were carefully chosen so they would remain secure when stacked. This kind of cribbing will never deteriorate or will never pollute the water (plate 44).

The well is bordered above the ground by a 2½'-high rock wall to minimize the danger of animals and humans falling into it. It is now covered with boards until I can make a hinged cover for it. The boards are a precaution against children climbing over the wall. The well was then enshrined with an unusual, rather oriental looking, shake roof to shade it in the summer, keep leaves from falling into it in autumn, and prevent snow from coming into it in winter. This roof is substantial and has a certain aesthetic appeal.

My idea, though not entirely clear at first, was to incorporate a shake pattern for the roof. From previous experience I found that shakes can have a somewhat sloppy look, especially around the eaves. I wanted to compensate for the "loppy-eared" look that I had been getting with the heavy shakes I've been using. So by building up the roof's eave support a little higher than would normally be the case, the first shakes went on in a near-horizontal position, but not enough to cause leakage. I found to my great surprise and satisfaction that the lower end of the second row of shakes came to rest, not on the upper part of the previous row as was usually the case, but near the center of those first shakes. In using this design, a realization dawned on me that I had discovered something about the way the oriental pagodas were made. I studied how I could develop the idea throughout the roof. It looked simple and proved to be. It was all a matter of common sense, but it took an eye for

44

LARGER ROCKS AT BOTTOM →

10

6'

BED ROCK

shaping the roof to one's taste. I couldn't wait to get each row of shakes on and see the effect. In order to fit the inner logic that was unfolding before me, the shake nailers had to become steeper as they went up. There was a functional reason for this design as well. The more pointed the roof peak the better it would shed the water, like the bow of a ship. The final step was to place an inverted, hollowed out log over the crack formed at the apex of the roof (plates 45 and 46).

After a few years of hard but gratifying work, with the blessing of a strong back and the necessary assistance from my wife and young children, I have come a long way toward accomplishing my primary "back to nature" objective. I have built all the necessary out buildings including a 5-ton capacity hay shed, a wood shed, a laundry house, a bunk house, and a chicken coop. I constructed a foot bridge which spans our early spring run off bed (plate 47) and made most of the furniture we need. I hand cleared over an acre and planted pasture grasses and legumes for the animals to graze on. We raise animals and fowl for meat, milk, eggs, and hides; plant a full garden each year for vegetables and fruit; cut our own firewood and cooking fuel; and do a bit of seasonal hunting. In short, we have developed for ourselves a new way of life; a life of hard, steady, year-in and year-out, satisfying physical work. And someday we hope to thereby achieve an even greater degree of self-sufficiency and self-reliance. Growing and

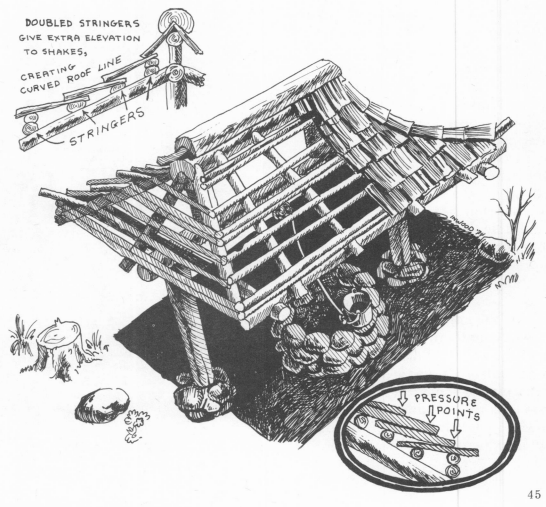

DOUBLED STRINGERS GIVE EXTRA ELEVATION TO SHAKES, CREATING CURVED ROOF LINE

STRINGERS

PRESSURE POINTS

45

processing our own clothing would be one
of the next very important steps in our
efforts to achieve these aims (plate 48).

What we have been doing on our land,
we feel must be done—not only for our
own good but, if only in a small way,
perhaps for the ultimate good. The results
of our labours are clear-cut and tangible.
As anyone knows who has made
something more or less original and
usable with his hands, such results give
an incomparable sense of personal
satisfaction. There is a New Testament
saying which lately I sometimes catch
myself quietly quoting as I am working:
"Ye shall know them by their works."

46

47

48

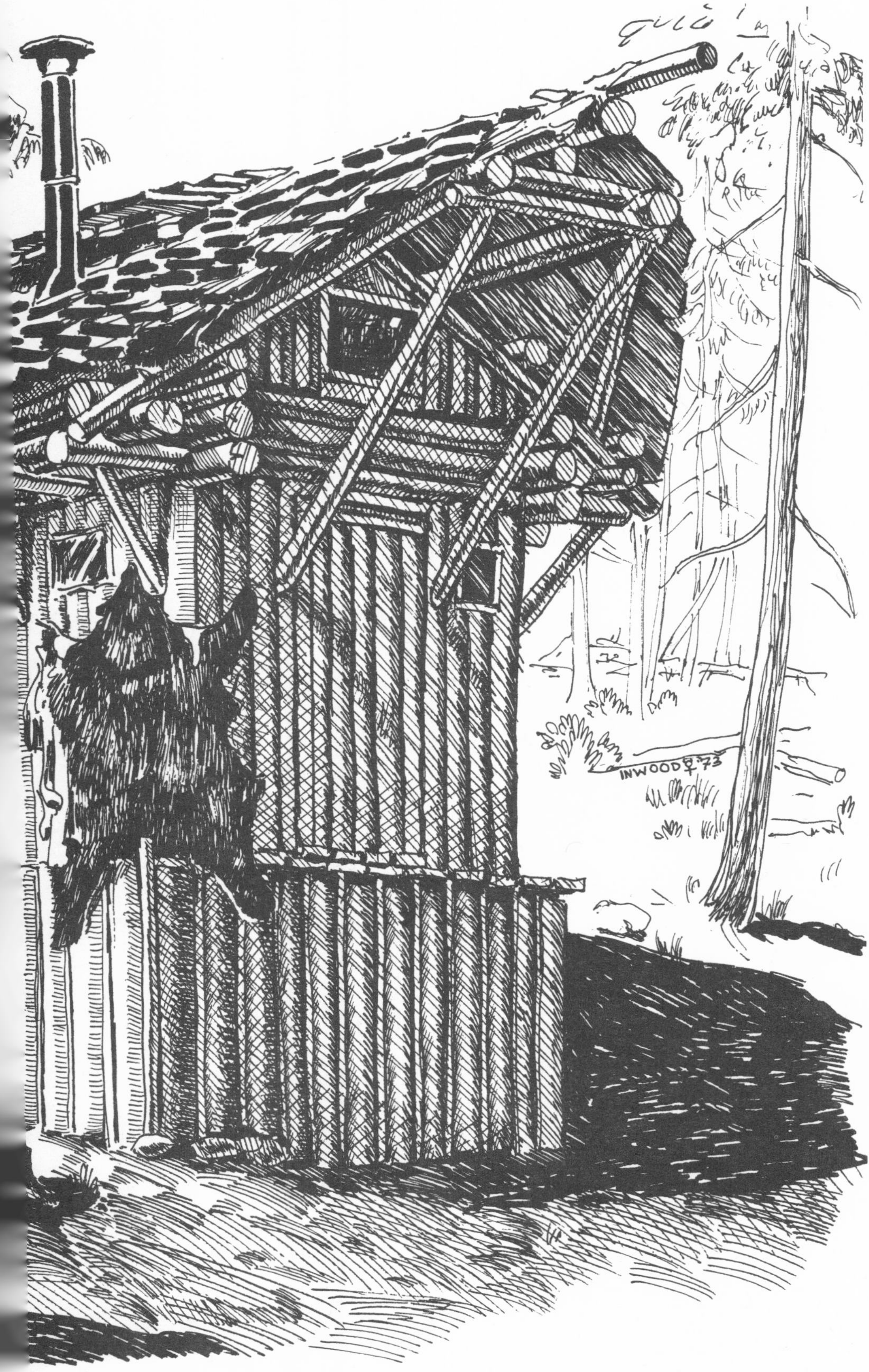
INWOOD '73

Spaces And Relationships

Instead of constructing this house themselves, the owners hired an architect to design it and basically inexperienced carpenters to build the structural portion of it. Yet they wanted their home to be special, something uniquely their own; most people want that. And being practicing artists, they desired their house to be aesthetically interesting in itself. To achieve that purpose, they put in the finishing touches, using the mediums they know best to enhance their home's structural beauty and make it a visible example of their own creative personalities.

Most architectural offices refuse to design small, individual houses because it is too much trouble for not enough profit. But there is usually a young architect around, a few years out of school, apprenticing in an office, who would love a chance to design a house (traditional moonlighting). The particular fellow they found was working as a night-shift janitor in a local pub when they hired him to design the house. In fact he did most of the designing in between his janitorial duties. He had "dropped out," as they used to say, leaving a large architectural corporation because he decided "it wasn't good for his health."

The owners wanted a two-bedroom house to fit their meager budget, so a design was developed that could be built in stages. The first stage was an octagon, 12′ on a side, about 30′ across. It would contain a completed kitchen and dining area, bathroom, sleeping loft, and living area. The living area would be temporarily partitioned off to provide a closed-in bedroom under the loft. The octagonal core would have one high, open ceiling space, and the areas would be divided by changes in floor levels, each level spiraling around the centerpole (plate 1). The first stage would be well within their budget.

The second stage would add a mudroom and a pantry at the entry, another bedroom, and a small, partially covered terrace deck off the kitchen. The partition in the living area would then be removed, and that space would double in size when the bedroom was added (plate 2). They chose to go this far with the structure at the beginning.

The third stage allowed for a large terrace off the living area and another bedroom which would extend from the east side of the octagonal core. This section could be built onto, almost indefinitely, as funds allowed (plate 3).

A site on a slope which provides complete southern exposure was chosen. It includes a view of the surrounding mountains and overlooks the nearby river (the river view has since become the sight for a huge canal project that wiped out its serene beauty). The southern exposure also provides the greatest amount of year-round sun.

Though the slope has a 6′ in 30 grade, it produced no problem. In fact it inspired the multileveled floor layout which follows the slope and sets the house into the landscape. A single-level floor design would have forced the house to be lifted out on cantilevers as an object that did not belong. In order to incorporate the structure to properly fit in with its surroundings, it had to be built as close to the ground as possible, making each level stay with the contour of the land (plates 4 and 5).

Since it was difficult for the owners, or anyone else without proper training, to visualize the architect's ideas from the drafting plans, the designer built a scale model of the house and explained its spaces and relationships. The house and its inner areas were positioned in relation to their exposure to the sun and the air flows. The southeast bedroom would get the cool, morning sun; the living area,

because of its southeastern, southern, and southwestern exposures would get the sun at different angles throughout the day; the dining area and kitchen, to the west and northwest, would get only the afternoon sun as it began setting behind the sparse forest behind these areas (plate 6).

3'-long eaves were designed to extend over the southern and western sections to shade them from the direct sun but allow sufficient light to enter through the many windows. The low, opening windows at the south, allow cool air to enter the house while higher vents let the warmer air escape.

From the standpoint of physical and personality elements, modification of standard building and designing practices were incorporated to fit the

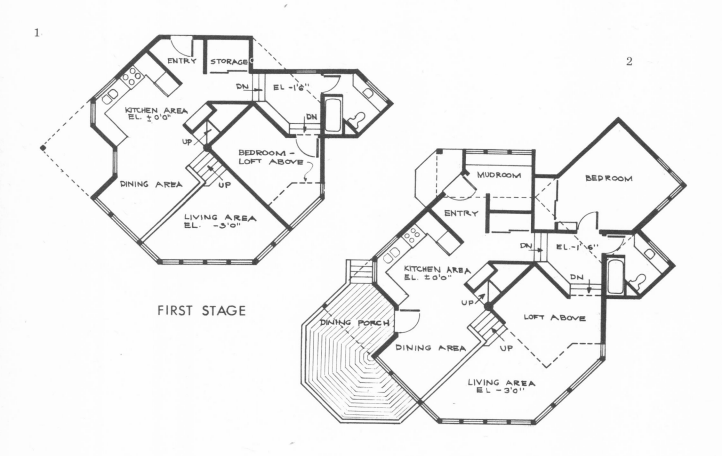

1.

FIRST STAGE

2

SECOND STAGE

owners. Because of Mr. Owner's height, which is 6′4″, the ceilings of each enclosed section were lifted 4″. High shelf spaces were allowed above closets and partitions for open storage of his pottery. The loft was designed as a semiprivate place for Mrs. Owner to do her writing. Many shelves were built into the loft railing for her books.

The whole central core has a spiralling effect around its centerpole axis. Each space moves into the next by natural progression, yet each is distinctly individual. The spaces are broken up for quietness and privacy by varying levels and short partitions. There are no dead ends within these areas.

The owners were pleased with the designer's concepts except for the lack of basement space. The site was wet in the springtime with runoff which flowed down from the background mountains. This made such a space impractical.

Construction started just after summer solstice, on June 22nd. The crew consisted of three relatively inexperienced builders and a master carpenter who visited the site every two weeks to aid in whatever problems arose and to give advice where needed. Joel headed the crew. Though he was not a journeyman carpenter himself, he had apprenticed under the master carpenter in the past. Mrs. Owner's son, was the second crew member. The

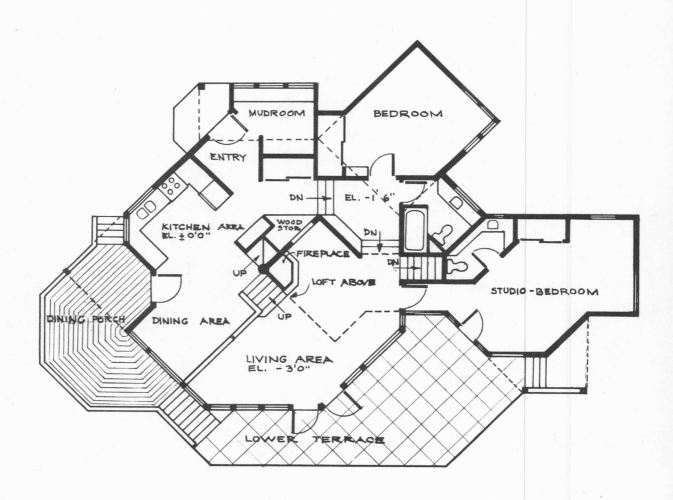

THIRD STAGE

designer was hired as the third member, to assist the others in carrying out his design. The trio and a few of their friends shared a bunk house, tents, and an old Doukhobor house which was on the property. They each received the same wage, $2.50 an hour. Rona became head cook and vegetable gardener, and though it was suggested that she too get equal pay, she refused the wage because she had no money for extra help. Everyone was involved on equal terms. The sense of building a truly creative structure as a communal effort made morale high.

The construction began with a traditional batter board and string layout, but because of the many angles of the octagonal core, it proved to be more difficult and complex than the usual. The builders roughed out an area approximately 12′ x 45′ and set up the batter boards at the four corners. Another rectangle, about 12′ x 30′ crossed the first

4

5

6

one, 8' from the southern end, making the basic octagonal shape. These rectangles were then checked to make sure they were true (plate 7).

After the area was laid out, an 18'-long trench, 3'-deep, was dug for a concrete block stabilizing wall. It ran southwest to northwest in the middle of the octagon where the central level change occurred. The stabilizing wall proved to be structurally unnecessary. The fireplace pad, which was incorporated in it, could have been made separately as an additional footing (*see* plate 7, center dotted lines).

Footing holes were dug at each of the 12 intersecting points of the octagon and at each angling point in the remaining sections—22 in all (*see* plate 9). Their holes were 3' deep to insure their being safely below the frost line. The forms only surrounded the 12" squares which protruded above the surface because the sandy ground below acted as a natural form for the rest.

The cement for the footings was poured. As the concrete began hardening, spikes, which would later be driven into the 6 x 6 upright posts that supported the floor beams, were sunk into the tops of the pads. The varying heights of the upright posts were determined by the surrounding terrain. If a footing was lower because the ground dipped, its post would be longer to compensate for it and to make it level. The posts have asphalt paper barriers below them to prevent the sweating concrete from prematurely rotting them (plate 8).

The design of this house incorporated three separate levels to keep the structure as close to the sloping ground as possible and to act as a space divider for the various areas. The living area and fire-nook floor is the lowest. 18" above it, is the bathroom, hall, and bedroom level. The kitchen, dining area, terrace, and

mudroom are on the upper deck, which is 18" higher than the second one, and 3' above the living area. To insure that each level would be as close to the contour of the slope as possible, joist hangers were used as needed. In areas such as the main bedroom, which is very near to the ground on the north end, the hangers make it possible to keep the joists at the same height as the floor beams, instead of lifting them 8" above these beams. Joist hangers are widely used and are known to be structurally sound.

The double 2 x 8 floor joists were spaced 16" at center and 4" of fiberglas insulation was tacked between them. A 1x subfloor was then nailed over them (*see* plate 9).

As the carpentry got more complex, the owners felt as if they were spectators to something that was running away from them rather than controllers of what was happening. Mr. Owner was teaching pottery at a nearby college and Mrs. Owner was growing vegetables, cooking for the crew, and working on her doctorate. The house seemed to be the private excitement of those who were working on it and did not seem to belong to the owners at all. In fact they found their own living quarters and privacy overrun by the crew and their occasional visitors who freely used the old house's facilities whenever they felt the need. At times, Walter even found it necessary to lock himself in the bathroom to escape the omnipresent crowd. What was happening on their own land was indeed a cultural shock to them. They were not used to living communally as they were forced into. But they could not complain; the work was going well. After all, how else would they get a custom job like this done for such a small monetary investment?

Next came the framing of the walls. The crew decided that the easiest and most accurate method of assembling each wall was to first lay out its pieces horizontally on the level deck, nail them together, then raise the finished frame and fix it into position. This method prevented tedious toe nailing and provided the carpenters with a straight surface on which they could line up and measure the 2 x 4's.

The studs were placed at 16″ centers and appropriate spaces were allowed for windows and doors. Where a window was to be put in, the cripples were cut to meet the horizontal sills. A cripple is any vertical stud which is interrupted by a horizontal piece before it spans the top and bottom plates. Single 2 x 4's were used to frame the windows and doorways. Any additional framing and spacers which absorb the settling of the completed structure were put in later.

The raised walls were plumbed with levels and the bottom plates were nailed through the subfloor to the floor beams. The wall sections were then joined together at the ends with flattened tin oil cans and they were capped with a second top plate of doubled 2 x 8's on end. The 2 x 8's lapped the first plates on the wall ends to provide an additional tie to keep the walls in place (plate 10).

Because most of the inside partitions were not bearing any structural load, they were framed with single studs, placed at 24″ centers, and were topped with single plates. When the framing was finished and the walls and partitions were in place, the once simple, visually appealing multilevel decks were transformed into a maze which looked like a forest with trees going every which way. There did not seem to be any continuity within the structure. But after the plywood sheathing was nailed on to the outside of the walls, the maze developed meaning. "Aha, there's the kitchen and the mudroom; this mess is really becoming a house."

After the decks, walls, and partitions

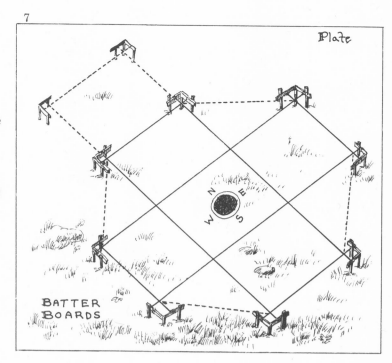

7

Plate

BATTER BOARDS

8

FOUNDATION POLE

TAR PAPER VAPOUR BARRIER

WOODEN FORM

PIN

CONCRETE FOUNDATION POURED INTO A FREEFORM CAVITY

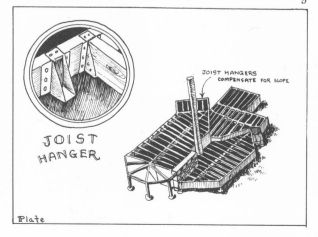

9

JOIST HANGER

JOIST HANGERS COMPENSATE FOR SLOPE

Plate

were in place it was time to provide the growing organism with a centerpole axis to support its roof and convert it into a spacial masterpiece. Along with the raising of that 16′ cedar pole came a welcomed celebration. As it was raised, cheers filled the air. The festive table was prepared by Mrs. Owner who was by then ready for anything. There was plenty of everything to make the celebrating last all night and it did. The bunk house and old house were filled with merry makers. Soon, exhausted by the event, Rona found her way to a quiet hillside and slept in the bracken (Mr. Owner was in the hospital "enjoying" an operation).

The next morning the weary crew began assembling the loft area. Spaces for the huge, custom-made beam hangers were cut into the centerpole. These hangers hold up two of the double 2 x 10 beams which frame the loft. Four of these beams surround the loft and span from the centerpole to the southern and southeastern walls. A ridge of 2 x 4's was nailed to the inside foot of the beams to support the heavy 4 x 6 double tongue-and-groove deck. A low railing was later placed around the loft area. A bookcase was then set into the front railing for Mrs. Owner's books (plate 11).

Before the actual construction began, Joel and the designer spent many hours trying to figure out a suitable roof support. One night Joel thought of airplane hangers and how those roofs were held up. After studying that type of truss system, he and the master carpenter designed a similar system which would intersect the original octagon and not detract from its open, spacial beauty by cluttering it with a network of ceiling joists.

The four trusses were hung from a fourway iron hanger located at the top of the centerpole. Each truss spans to opposite walls. Their main function is to hold up the collar beams which form a 12′ square around the centerpole to brace the roof. Two of the trusses also act as gigantic hip rafters which support the hip roofs. The other pair are hip rafters until they meet the collar beams, then they continue as ridge boards for the gables over the front door and loft areas. Each has two double 2 x 6 frames with webbing bolted between each side (plates 12 and 13).

10

Loft Area
Plate 11

12

13

The roof in this dwelling is many-layered. The interior roof is made up of 2 x 6 nailers which are spaced at 36" centers. These nailers are visible from the interior and span from the collar beams outward. Not only do they enhance the spiral effect of the ceiling, but they also act as nailing strips for the materials above. This gives the carpenters the advantage of not having to nail upward from below; instead they comfortably work from above. That feature alone justifies the extra use of materials. The nailing boards also provide a deceptive sense of structure which confuses even skilled carpenters. From the interior they look like rafters placed too far apart which hold up an uninsulated cedar ceiling.

After the interior nailing boards were in place, the 1 x 8 ceiling was put on. Economy grade cedar at $40 per 1000 board feet was bought for this job. The usable, unrotten and unsplit sections of each board were sawed out and nailed up. The rest was used above the outer rafters to nail the shakes onto. Nothing was wasted. The cedar 1 x 's were spaced 3/8" apart to allow for shrinkage. Since shrinkage is inevitable, the spacing is a method of developing uniformity in the sizes of spaces between the boards (plate 14).

When the ceiling was finished, the designer laid on the loft floor and studied the fissures of light which shone in through the spaces between the boards. He watched as they seemed to spin around the centerpole, giving the roof the desired spherical appearance. To finish the ceiling, the shining light had to be shut out. A layer of black building paper was stapled to the boards to cover them and act as a temporary vapour seal until the finish roof was put on.

The outer 2 x 6 hip rafters and ridge boards were cut and placed. The roof rafters were then spaced at 24" centers,

nailed over the ceiling, and supported at the outer walls, collar beams, and hip rafters. The angle to which each rafter was cut depended on the pitch of the roof and the angles of intersection with the ridge rafters. The rafters and ridge boards extended 3' beyond the walls as eaves to shade the interior and protect the exterior lap siding from direct precipitation.

Blocking was put in between each rafter directly above the collar beams to keep the long, spanning rafters from spreading. Six inches of fiberglas insulation was then tacked between the rafters. Though some may think this thickness is unnecessary and prevents air circulation, the roof is excellently insulated and the snow does not melt on it, preventing damage from ice collection.

The 1x cedar scraps left over from the ceiling material were nailed across the rafters to support the finish roof of cedar shakes. The 24" shakes used on the roof were store-bought, but they could easily be made from cedar bolts (see chapter 6). The shakes were lined up on the cedar nailing strips which were spaced 6" apart as in the chapter 3 example (plates 15 and 16).

Normal preparation for plumbing and electricity was made before the interior 1 x 6 cedar ship-lap paneling was nailed on. It was then time to begin the interior finishing. Very little money was left, and the crew decided it was time to depart. The coming months of severe winter made it impossible to work. The following spring, the owners, and their daughter became more involved in the house and finally felt it was theirs. They learned to use hammers and saws. They put up most of the plywood and became skillful in paneling with cedar.

For a long while, they could not decide on the material they were going to use for the finish floors. Mr. Owner was creative and employed the art form he knew best.

In Harmony with Nature   137

17

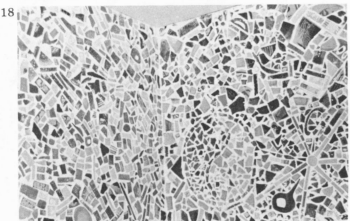

18

19

It took 500 pounds of clay to make the unglazed tiles which he used, but it could have taken more had he not left the plywood and subflooring under the carpets untiled (plate 17).

He also made copper-red glazed-tile counters for the kitchen and bathroom. His wife is finishing off the bathroom shower area in a tile mosiac made mostly of unsatisfactory pots hammered into pieces in the potter's tradition (plate 18). Not everyone is a potter, but most people have some special skill. Many other materials could be used for the finishing touches.

The designer is pleased with the way the owners incorporated their own talents and imagination into the house. It would never have occurred to him to use hand-made tiles for the finish flooring or make cupboards out of the same paneling as that of the rest of the interior.

This wood house, built into the slope, succeeds in becoming a masterpiece of *spaces and relationships* and blends well with its backgrounding forest and mountains. Its gabled roof entranceway protects one from the weather even before he enters into the backlit mudroom area where he may remove his overcoat and kick off his shoes. The spaces beyond the entrance foyer are shielded by a partition. From above this shield, the centerpost, trusses, and livingroom lights can be seen. People can be heard from those areas. One has time to become oriented and choose his route. To the right, past the open cupboard featuring many of Mr. Owner's useful ceramics (plate 19), is the kitchen. To the left, down to a lower level, is the bathroom and bedroom.

The kitchen is an open area with windows that frame the hillside apple orchard and expose a narrow corridor into the woods (plate 20). From this area one can see into the dining area which is only divided from the kitchen by its own rectangular shape and its different floor (plate 21). From here one can also look out the high windows of the lower living area.

Between the dining and kitchen spaces there is a dutch door which leads out to the roofed section of the terrace, past the west wall. The terrace is partially covered by the end of a hip roof. Its open deck extends from the west wall out to a railing which will soon be sheathed-in with cedar siding to protect it from low breezes. The terrace overlooks the large backgrounding mountain range and a nearby stand of aspens (plates 22 and 23).

20

21

22

The afternoon sunlight streams in through the many windows of the dining area and makes the huge, carved wood table glow within this space. This table is where Mrs. Owner chooses chooses to do most of her writing. This space is divided by a short partition and a few steps which lead to the lower living area (plate 24). One can stand at the partition and view the whole lower area or sit at the table and feel completely closed off from it. From the living area, the spiraling ceiling and the large, spanning trusses seem to be much higher up than they really are. The many windows which surround the area make them seem so (plate 25).

Beside the living area is another space about the same size. Yet because of its low ceiling, it gives the sensation of being much smaller. This area is a fire nook which will soon be enhanced with a beautiful brick and clay fireplace (plate 26).

The upper loft towers over the other levels and allows one to look down from its sides and see the spaces of the basic octagonal core. When standing, one could even gaze out of the high living area windows which parallel one's vision. When sitting, he would be in a private space provided by the encompassing railings (plates 27 and 28).

Two other separate areas with closing doors are additions to the original octagonal core. The bathroom is a tiny, five-cornered room, fully equipped with bath, shower, sink, and toilet. The wall behind the bath-shower is decorated with the tile mosaic which Mrs. Owner is still piecing together. The sink has a copper glazed-tile counter. For the purpose of viewing the upper meadow, the toilet is

23

24

25

26

In Harmony with Nature   141

located in the center of the room, facing the window (plate 29).

The adjoining bedroom has a shed roof which slants down away from the octagonal core. Its gyprock walls break the cedar paneling style and help to make this room different from the rest of the house.

This structure is now being lived in by its owners. They are delighted with its views and are very comfortable within its spaces. They feel it is truly a house tailor-made for themselves and they regret that they did not participate as much as they could have in the actual building of it. They discovered that it is more worthwhile making something you want, than to earn money with your time so you can pay someone else to make it for you (plates 29 and 30).

27

29

28

8

For many years I worked at an office job in my native country, Germany. As I used to sit at my desk, easing my mind from the piles of paperwork in front of me, I would sometimes look out at the harbor and wish I could trade places with the dock workers. I wanted to feel the weight of one of their large crates on my shoulder and walk to the waiting cargo ships with the heavy container. But instead of doing something about that foolish desire, I just went to the coffee machine, refilled my cup, and forgot about such wild fantasies.

I soon became very restless and realized something was missing in my life. My body was trying to hint its needs to me. I was usually very tense and had many unexplained aches and pains. But as my body cried out, I quieted it with aspirins or alcohol. I became more sluggish and knew something was wrong. I began asking myself many questions like: "Was my body designed to sit all day at a desk and push papers around?"

I began reading about my body and how it functioned. I read about disease germs and how they collect and reproduce in parts of the body which get very little circulation. I learned that natural resistance breaks down with lack of body movement and that a person needs plenty of exercise to maintain good health. I became aware of myself as a human animal who was meant to be outdoors, using his muscles as well as his mind to sustain his existence.

That awareness was the important factor that made me change my lifestyle. I picked up whatever literature I could find about living in the country and surviving on a homestead. My dream was to meet all my needs in such an environment without having to waste many precious hours each day working in an office or at some other form of unsatisfying servitude.

My first step toward my dream was to travel around and find the place I wanted to spend the next several years developing. It had to be a place that allowed me enough personal freedom to experiment with my ideas and reap the benefits. Though there is nowhere in this world that one can find such total freedom, I am happy to say I stumbled upon an area which is a satisfactory compromise. And here is where I met the beautiful, hard working woman who shared the same fantasies and decided to soon share her home with me as well.

Our homestead is located in the foothills near a high range of mountains. It provides us with good soil, plenty of fresh water, varying terrains, and privacy. It reminds me of many areas in the Alps which I enjoyed visiting. In fact I used much of the information I learned from Alpine farmers everyday as I was planning our homestead. Those farmers always built their homes and the animal quarters on the hillsides, leaving the flatland open for farming and gardening. The grazing fields were also on the slopes, so the nutrients of the animal manure would wash down onto the produce fields.

The barns were dug into those slopes to provide the animals with warm, earthen stables which were beneath the ground level on the uphill side and exposed on the downhill side. Of course such stables needed to be well ventilated. Another advantage to this design is that hay and grain can easily be unloaded into the upper loft which is level to the ground on the uphill side (plate 1).

Our house is also built into a small hillside and has very good drainage on either side because it is sheltered by the long, overhanging roof which straddles the crest of the hill. It has a full 27 x 27 basement which was dug out by a caterpillar tractor. I wanted such a basement as a workshop area and a place for a root cellar where we could preserve some of our garden and field produce for the winter. A refrigerator just could not keep all that we needed to store. Besides, we did not want to have to depend on expensive electricity.

If there is time and means, it is a very good idea to build the root cellar under the house, then there is only one roof to worry about. There is no need for additional insulation above the cellar because very little, if any, warmth travels

1

down to it from the living section on the upper level. If the root cellar is built into the slope, like the animal stable, it should be deep into the ground on the uphill side and level with it on the downhill side, enabling the gardener to just wheelbarrow the produce in through the front door.

In our design, the 20 x 27 workshop is on the downhill side of the 7 x 27 root cellar, protecting it from the weather and insulating it. The long, overhanging roof which straddles the crest above also protects the cellar because it detours the runoff, preventing it from collecting around and penetrating through the rammed-earth walls of the basement area. Even with this roof, the root cellar still retains all the natural moisture of the earth just as does an ideal garden, because it is underground (plate 2).

It is important to only build into the slope of a small hill when that hill's crest can be covered with such a straddling roof. If a structure is built into the bottom or at a lower part of a large hill or mountain, the hole for that structure will usually create a spring which will penetrate any concrete basement unless its walls are thoroughly tarred and have a water barrier of gravel or clay tile around their footings. I have seen such cellars in $20,000 contractor-built houses with 2′ of water in them at spring breakup.

The retaining wall around a basement which was set into a slope like ours can be made of rammed earth (soil cement) since there is no danger of runoff to wash it away. Rammed earth is an inexpensive soil mixture, usually made up of 60% sand and 40% clay-type soil.

WOOD STORAGE

ROOTCELLAR

WORKSHOP AREA

INWOOD '74

2

It is held together with about 7% Portland cement. If rammed earth is used for fill between heavy post and beam walls it can contain clay, straw, small twigs, even sawdust, and it will just require a small amount (no less than 7%) of concrete to cement it all together. A wall of this sort should be protected by a roof overhang of at least 2½' to prevent direct moisture from eroding it.

Rammed earth is more economical and insulates much better than an equal amount of concrete. It has a thermal quality which makes it remain cool in summer and helps it to retain heat in the winter. A 10″ thickness of rammed earth, 60% sand and 40% clay with 7% Portland cement as a retaining wall can easily support a single-story dwelling with a heavy snow load. We used this standard mixture for our basement walls.

We started by putting in a form for the footing around two sides of the perimeter of the basement. The form was made from 1 x 6 boards, two-high, which were braced at the corners and every 4' with 2 x 4 uprights that were buried 1' into the ground. They extended 8' high for the full length walls and were held together at the top with twisted wires.

The rammed earth mixture is a drier one than regular concrete. The mortar should be moist enough to mix properly but be crumbly to the touch. It should not slump when it is worked a bit by hand. When the mortar was the proper consistency, it was shoveled into the footing form. It was tamped down with an eight-pound sledge hammer until it pressed into every part of the form and the excess mortar oozed out of the corners. It was then left to set, with

2″x 4″ BRACES ARE DRIVEN INTO GROUND & KEPT FROM SPREADING WITH WIRE OR 1″x SCRAP BRIDGING THEM

OPTIMUM TAMPING TOOL IS 3″ METAL SQUARE WELDED ONTO LENGTH OF PIPE

3

pieces of rebar sticking out every 18″ to join with the retaining walls (plate 3).

I began building the forms for the north and south walls and realized that I would have a problem securing them above the footing pads. But I figured that because of the dryness of the mortar, not much would ooze out from under the forms when it was tamped down. The 1 x 6 boards were raised to 36″ at these walls. They, too, were braced at every 4′ with 2 x 4's, and this bracing was supported by the longer uprights which framed the footing forms. To tie the walls together, I placed bent, hewn timber uprights at each corner over the footings. These uprights also acted as nailing posts for the form ends. Their bends lean in toward the building to give the walls added structural strength. I raised the forms 36″ because this height is a comfortable one for the first tamping and it is also where the windows will be started on the south and east walls. The north wall will be a full wall without windows.

By the time that I got around to building the form for the west retaining wall, which is the wall furthest into the slope behind the root cellar, I decided to try a different style. I built the forms so the inside of this cellar wall would slope like a dam. It would be 10″ wide on top and slant to a width of 24″ at the footing. This wedge- or dam-shaped wall is much stronger than the ordinary straight wall and is easier to make. It does not have to be supported on a footing because its thickness is relative to the amount of back pressure it might receive.

After the rammed earth was tamped

BACK FILLED AFTER FORM WAS REMOVED

BOW IN BACK RETAINING WALL FORM MADE BY USING 2″ x 10″ PLANKS, RIPPED ALONG ONE EDGE TO THE DESIRED CURVATURE

BACK OF LOG PAINTED WITH TAR EMULSION

RE-BAR SUNK INTO SIDE WALLS TIE INTO REAR RETAINING WALL

① ② ③ order in which foundation walls were formed

in and the completed retaining wall was left to set, the 8 x 8 timber window sills were notched into the end posts over the 3' wall sections of the south and east walls. An 8 x 8 upright support was placed between each window space to frame it in. These uprights also act as structural posts for the top wall beams which were notched in above them. Five windows were then put into the south wall, and four windows and a door went into the east wall to bring in plenty of light to the shop area. Work benches were built under these windows and other wood-work conveniences will soon be added. (Plate 4).

I did not want to put a cement floor in the workshop because I do not like to walk on such floors. For the present, the floors in both the workshop and the root cellar are dirt with a few wood chips mixed in. I am thinking of sinking some joist beams between porous gravel and nailing a rough 1x floor over them. The gravel will provide drainage between the joists and prevent them from prematurely rotting (plates 5–8).

6

7

5

The two root-cellar sections are separated from the workshop area by an 8"-thick insulated double wall. The insulation used between the walls is oat straw which had been bathed in an asphalt emulsion. This emulsion is a very effective and long lasting mixture of three fungus-retarding agents: asphalt, lime, and water-glass silicate. (It only cost us $12 for a 45-gallon drum, 1968 prices). I submerged the straw into the emulsion, left it in the sun to dry, then pressed the treated straw in between the walls with my fists.

The root-cellar sections are divided by a rammed-earth wall. On the north side of the wall there is a shelved area for the storage of canning jars, crocks of sauerkraut, sacks of potatoes, a barrel of eggs, and the more delicate produce like apples. Apples are not supposed to

8

be mixed with the odorous vegetables like cabbage and onions because they will end up tasting like them.

At that time, we preserved the eggs by mixing in a solution of waterglass silicate to the water in the barrel. This nontoxic chemical compound turns the water into a gelatinous mass that reduces the capillary action of the liquid to prevent air from entering the barrel and spoiling the eggs. An old, nearby farmer told us of a simpler method that we now use. He mixes lime with salt and puts the two ingredients into the barrel of liquid. The mixture produces a diluted, mortarlike substance that coats and seals the eggs, keeping them fresh for several weeks at a time.

The south area of the root cellar has a 2½'-high bin that is filled with sand. Carrots and beets are buried in between the layers of sand. This preserves them throughout the winter as if they were still in the ground. The various crops like cabbage and brussel sprouts were harvested with their root systems attached and were replanted into the moist earthen floor. This method of retaining their freshness works well because the roots think they are still in the soil and continue to supply the plants with life sustaining nutrients.

There are four holes, 14" deep in this south cellar for milk. We placed old flue linings in these holes and put in the containers of milk. The milk keeps cold enough in these linings to stay fresh for several days. The milk even feels cold to my teeth after being in the holes for many hot summer days.

Though the walls of these cellars remain dry, they receive enough moisture from their soil floors to keep them cool. For proper circulation, they have air vents near their ceilings to allow the warm, rising air to escape. These 8 x 8 x 16 cement blocks are built into the north and west walls. The cool air comes in from the workshop and pushes the old, musty air out through the high vents. Root cellars need this type of vent system to prevent mold and fungi from forming in the otherwise stagnant dampness (plate 9).

After the basement walls were finished, 28'-long fir joists were put in over them. They spanned between the east and west walls. The joist ends that rested above the west wall were tarred and cemented onto that wall with the rammed-earth mixture. This provided a flat surface for the living area wall plate and floor to rest on. It also gave the building added sheer strength. Many of the rough 1 x 6 boards that were used as the retaining wall forms were nailed over the joists as a subfloor for the upper area (plate 10).

On the uphill side of the slope we can walk from ground level, through the wood shed, and into the living section. Here again, I used some techniques I learned from the Alpine farmers. Our walls were post-and-beam with modified rammed-earth mixture as the filler. The triangular bracing for these walls is a variation of styles used in this type of construction in Germany.

The posts were made from cedar logs which I hewed to 8″ square at the site where they were cut so the horse would not have to drag any excess weight. I used cedar because it is the most porous of the local woods. Being porous, it is rot resistant, light in weight, and also very insulative. I hewed these timbers by first chopping a score cut against the grain every 1′ or so with an axe. If the wood had a very straight grain, which

9

ENDS OF JOISTS PAINTED WITH CREOSOTE AND TAR

10

11

most large cedar logs do, the score cuts could be spaced further apart. I used a coarse adze or a broadaxe and made them roughly square (plate 11). At the building site I finished the 8″ squares with a ship builder's adze.

The posts were spaced along the south wall according to the width of the windows we had. We bought 94 old 4 x 2 and 3½ x 2 framed windows for $2 each. We wanted at least four of the 4 x 2 windows along the south wall to bring in the sunlight throughout the year. There is something very romantic about waking up on a cold winter morning to the bright sunshine reflecting off the white snow-covered landscape. It really helps to start the day off right. And to me light is worth more than warmth. I spend a lot of time outdoors and enjoy it when the outside can come inside by way of large window spaces. The Japanese say that light is very necessary for comfort. Dark spaces are depressing; light spaces bring out inner happiness.

After the posts were toe nailed onto the bottom wall plates, they were braced with slightly curved diagonal braces. These braces were hewed from bent cedar pieces to add an aesthetic touch to the walls. In European post-and-beam architecture, there are sometimes many bracing designs used to break up the monotony of similar diagonal patterns going around the whole building. Three common patterns are Der Mann, Der Woman, Der Wild Mann (plate 12). My design was much simpler; the aesthetic beauty being in the curved pieces that I hand hewed (plate 13).

The window sills and the top beam were not put in place until after the rammed earth was tamped in. Otherwise they would have been obstacles during that process. To prepare the posts for the rammed earth and to prevent air

DER MANN   DER WOMANN   DER WILDEMANN

12

spaces when the mortar dries and
contracts, I attached 1 x 1 strips of board
to the outside and inside edges of the
posts. An inside wall form of plywood,
to the height of the window sill, was
then nailed to the posts and two 1 x 6
boards were nailed to the outside.

A rammed-earth mortar, consisting
of five parts sawdust, 5 parts sand, and
1 part Portland Cement was mixed very
dry (moist to the touch but crumbly)
for the walls. People said this mixture
wouldn't last because the sawdust would
soon rot out, but I remembered reading
about sawdust and cement floors in
1895 Victory-type ships. It worked for
those ships; why couldn't it work for my
walls? It in fact does work very fine;
probably because the Portland cement
contains lime which prevents fungi from
forming on the sawdust. This mixture
was pushed between the forms and
tamped down with the sledge hammer
(plates 14 and 15).

8″ of a rammed-earth mixture of this
type gives more insulation than an equal
thickness of regular cement, because
it is more porous and contains many
tiny dead air spaces like a hollow cinder

13

In Harmony with Nature   155

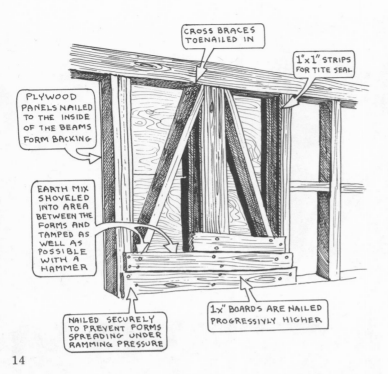

PLYWOOD PANELS NAILED TO THE INSIDE OF THE BEAMS FORM BACKING

CROSS BRACES TOENAILED IN

1"x1" STRIPS FOR TITE SEAL

EARTH MIX SHOVELED INTO AREA BETWEEN THE FORMS AND TAMPED AS WELL AS POSSIBLE WITH A HAMMER

NAILED SECURELY TO PREVENT FORMS SPREADING UNDER RAMMING PRESSURE

1x" BOARDS ARE NAILED PROGRESSIVLY HIGHER

14

block. It is durable enough for filling in between posts and beams, because it does not have to carry any structural weight and will last quite a long time if a certain precaution is taken—this precaution being that the roof directly above the wall have an overhang of at least 2½' to prevent direct precipitation from eroding it.

We are very happy with the way the south wall came out. It is aesthetically pleasing and it gives us a very fine view. There is of course plenty of light coming in from its 16 feet of window space. In fact just below the windows inside the house we have a wide sill for starting plants or sprouting grain and seeds. We even have a continuous oat sprouter, made from a hollowed out log, on a slight slant. It sprouts oats by the bucketful for chicken feed, resulting in dark orange egg yolks in the middle of the winter. This sprouter is warmed by a couple of hot bricks, exchanged twice daily and reheated on the wood stove (plates 16 and 17).

15

WOODEN MATRIX SECURES EARTH FILLING TO FRAME

EARTH FILL MIX CONSISTS OF: CLAY - STRAW and MANURE of modeling clay consistency

OLDE EUROPEAN STYLE EXPOSED BEAM BUILDING

The southern half of the west wall is also rammed-earth filled post-and-beam. This wall is level with the crest of the hill and is protected by a long overhanging roof that covers the woodshed in front of it. The entrance of the living area is located here under the 14' overhangs (plate 18).

The northern half of the west wall, the north, and east walls are frame construction with 2 x 4 studding and cedar 1x sheathing. They were insulated with asphalt-emulsion treated straw as was the inner wall to the root cellar. This treated straw is proving to be a very good insulation. It provides the walls with a lightweight, porous sealer that contains many dead air spaces which effectively keep out the cold and retain the heat (plate 19).

For our chimney, we made a concrete pad above the rammed-earth wall which divides the root cellar compartments. We used two commercial 8 x 8 flue linings and mortared in red bricks around them, filling in any spaces that were between the bricks and linings. Near the bottom of the chimney we left one brick loose in front of the lining opening to clean out the creosote. To make sure we were secured against chimney fires, we wanted a solid brick chimney instead of just having stove pipe going out through the wall. Many people I know and have heard about have lost their homes due to creosote buildup that finally caught fire in a flimsy stove pipe. The fire then ignited with either their cedar shake roofs or framed ceiling (plate 20).

Throughout the open living area there are a few 6 x 6 upright posts which brace the horizontal rafter supports and hold up the roof. These uprights relieve the roof pressure on the walls and prevent them from spreading under the weight of a snow load. In the center there is also a 22'-long centerpost which spans from a pier on the shop floor to the peak of the roof. The upright supports are spaced approximately 9' on-center, bracing the peak and going

16

17

18

north and south across the east floor. They are directly over crossing floor joists. Since the roof peak is off-center, there is no need for upright supports on the west side because the rafters span less than 11′ between the peak and the west wall.

Notched in above the posts, going north and south, are the 6 x 6 horizontal rafter supports. They are braced to the uprights by diagonal wind stiffeners. These wind stiffeners are curved pieces of log that add another aesthetic touch to the interior of the house. Their structural purpose is to prevent the walls from parallelagraming or collapsing because of unexpected heavy winds. All the natural forces that want to destroy a structure attack the roof except for the wind. Wind has been known to destroy many buildings that would otherwise be sound but lack bracing against its unexpected force (plates 21–23).

19

20

21

2 PIECE RIDGEPOLE

22

INWOOD '77

The center ridgebeam is not one continuous timber, but two separate pieces. These pieces were spliced with a side-lap joint and were bolted together. They were then supported from underneath by a short beam which spans between the two nearest uprights. This support beam is braced by two diagonals, securing it to the posts. The ridgebeam spans 3' beyond the north and south walls, providing them with plenty of overhang for protection (plates 24 and 25).

Because I was working with 5"-diameter and larger poles and did not plan on using store-bought insulation for the roof, I spaced my rafters at roughly 28" on-center. This rafter placement is sufficient to carry a heavy snow load since the rafters are braced in the center of their span by the crossing support beams. The rafters on the east side of the building are pine and larch because these types of wood have very little taper. They span from above the center cross-beam to 5' over the east wall. This overhang protects the lower entrance way below and detours the runoff so it won't come near the basement retaining wall.

The rafters on the west side are cedar because they only span a short distance from the offcentered peak to the west wall. Since these rafters overhang 14' beyond that wall to cover the outside wood shed and shield the crest of the hill from runoff, they have to be more weather resistant than the others. Cedar, though it usually tapers drastically, is the most weather resistant of all the local species of wood. Since these rafters only span a short distance inside the house, their tapers are not very noticeable.

Our subroof is a double thickness of slab boards which are on the average about 6"-wide. The second layer laps over the sides of the first as do roof shakes. The boards of these two layers are spaced half their width apart to create dead air corridors between them. When these corridors are properly sealed off, they effectively insulate the roof because they are not exposed to outside weather. And since the air is trapped in these areas, much of the rising heat from the house cannot pass through them. Instead it is locked between the boards and is not lost through the roof. Of course there is some heat loss but not enough to prevent our house from staying toasty when our wood stove is going.

Above the two layers of slab boards there is a sheet of aluminum builder's foil, shiny side down, to reflect the ultraviolet heat rays which have come through the air spaces. This foil barrier holds in much of the otherwise escaping heat and is well worth its nominal price. A continuous layer of 1x boards was then nailed over the aluminum foil to provide a flat surface for the finish roofing of rolled 90-weight asphalt paper (plate 25).

This style of subroof gives us about the same insulation as would 3½″ of fiberglas and is far less expensive. But even with 3½″ of fiberglas insulation, there would still be some heat loss, resulting in the snow melting on the roof and icing up at the eaves. We have this problem now. When the snow melts and collects on the eaves the mass of ice will travel upward by capillary action and back up under the eaves, thus entering into the house and dripping through the subroof. To prevent this ice buildup, we protected our eaves with an 18″-wide flashing of aluminum. The ice slides off this flashing instead of building up over it (plate 27).

We have a skylight built into the roof over the kitchen area. This skylight was easy to install. It was framed much like a window casing, except more care was taken to seal

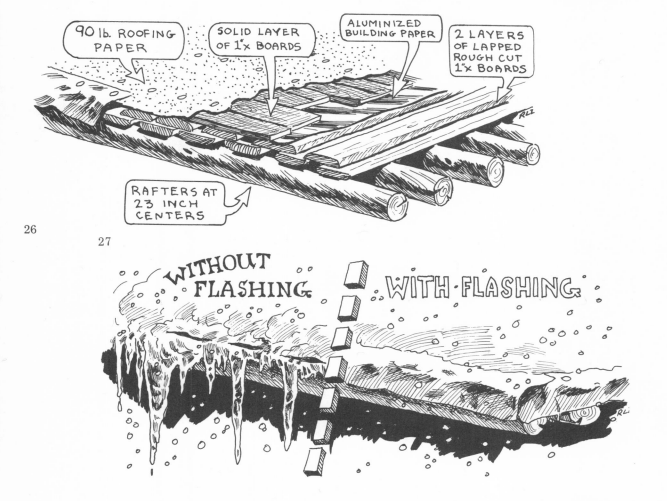

90 lb. ROOFING PAPER

SOLID LAYER OF 1″x BOARDS

ALUMINIZED BUILDING PAPER

2 LAYERS OF LAPPED ROUGH CUT 1″x BOARDS

RAFTERS AT 23 INCH CENTERS

26

27

WITHOUT FLASHING

WITH·FLASHING

28

this frame so no water vapour would seep through. A very good way to seal such a frame is to cover all the joints with tar. Also make sure that the window you use is of a substance that will not shatter or break under a heavy snow load. We used tinted corrugated plastic. It is working fine and is much cheaper than a safe thickness of glass (plate 28).

As a finishing touch to the roof, my wife hollowed out a thin cedar pole to be used as a trough at the edge of the north eave. This ingenious device keeps water from randomly dripping off that eave and splashing on whoever is walking under it. It also controls the flow of the melting snow and allows us to collect it in a barrel for domestic use when our water system freezes, which it does occasionally in the dead of winter (plates 29 and 30).

We are very comfortable in our little house and are especially pleased with the light-giving south wall. In fact we still have not curtained it off with the woven drapery my wife has been producing on her loom. If we have any regret to the design of our house it would be in the roof. If we had it to do over again, with the proper amount of money of course, we would put in 6″ of fiberglas or the equivalent thereof. This would control the heat loss and keep our house even toastier throughout the winter with the minimal of cord-wood cutting energy. But then again, cutting wood keeps one healthy during the long dormant winter.

We are finding, through the experience of the last few years here, that trying to maintain an almost self-sufficient homestead is a full-time job and often motivates more physical, mental, and emotional energy than we are sometimes willing to put out. But I must also add, the rewards are many and the faith we have been gaining in our personal resourcefulness in solving life problems is well worth the energy we are giving. *Energy given is energy received* (plates 31 and 32).

EAVE TROUGH FROM A
HOLLOWED OUT CEDAR POLE

29

30

31

32

INWOOD '73

Difficulty in the Beginning: It Furthers One To Appoint Helpers

$225 a month for a two-story, termite-ridden, cesspool stinking rural ratshed with bees buzzing in the chimney, gas leaks in the kitchen, and water so soapy that it sudded by itself in the sink. We were satisfied there though until the nearby city's smog penetrated through the mountains and putrified the once pure air. With it came the tourists and the traffic checks and the tickets and the helicopter harrassment. It was time for us to move on. We had a little money so we decided to maybe lose ourselves in the high plateaus of Peru and ski the Andes until the money ran out. But first we wanted to visit our friends who had recently escaped to the North Land. They would surely enjoy sharing our negative sanctions and complaints about the "old country". It would reinforce their belief in their new wilderness struggle.

When we got to their homestead we expected them to relate their hardship in trade for ours. But though they were living out of a temporary one-week wonder which they built out of scrap lumber, and the temperature was just above freezing, they had nothing but good to say about their new home. All was going well for them. They were working together for something they believed in. They loved the peacefulness of their riverfront forest and would not trade it for anything.

Instead of our laying our bummers on them, they began teaching us new things. They showed us edible mushrooms and plants that grew wild which were there for the taking. They showed us the forest and told us their plans for a new log house. Before long we helped them cut and peel logs and prepare the firewood.

Our friends, like us, did not have any knowledge of building with logs or any other material, being city dwellers. But they were determined to build their log house. It seemed like within hours after the project had started, many neighbors, both old-timers and new "textbook pioneers", offered their assistance. Some of them helped physically and some expounded theories over homemade elderberry wine. We couldn't believe the cooperation and helpfulness of these people. They were truly neighbors.

After working with our friends for awhile and learning from some of their mistakes and experiences, we decided that this area would be a fine place to settle. The folks were really friendly and the valley, surrounded by large mountains, was very beautiful and protective.

We searched for a short while and soon located an old homestead complete with house, barn, root cellar, and out buildings. Our vacation money went for the down payment on the place—so much for South America for the time being.

Soon after we moved in, the roofs of the old barn and storehouse collapsed. We examined the remains of the barn and found that most of the massive 12″-to16″ diameter cedar logs which comprised its walls had decayed into rotted pulp, good only for composting. We invited a few neighbors to help demolish the structure and shared whatever firewood we could salvage.

The root cellar was the next to go. The only thing usable from that mess was the concrete front. The rest went to the dump.

At least we could live in the house for a while. It is still sound. It has no actual foundation just a few rock piles it rests on. Its walls and floors slant in various directions, but it is warm and cozy—and the price was right.

We really got into the rural frame of mind fast. We wanted to immediately become self-sufficient and raise all sorts of useful animals. We bought a horse for riding and doing farm work (we thought). We got a black angus heifer for milk and meat breeding, and goats for immediate milk. Since the winters are cold in this area the first construction project was to build a log barn to house this menagerie. I wanted to try building with log primarily because of its rustic beauty, and secondly, because it is plentiful in our area and there are many sections of land that could use a little selective thinning out.

We have an adequate wood lot on our land, yet we wanted to get the logs for the structure elsewhere for the time being. A neighbor from across the river needed some land cleared. He made me a proposition I couldn't refuse. If we would clear the land for him and raise his pig along with ours (yes, pigs too) until it was ready to be slaughtered, he would let us keep all the tamarack we needed for the barn. He suggested we use tamarack because of its durability and straightness. We found that it was also a very easy wood to work with because it had few limbs or knots except near the top.

We trucked the logs to the barn site and immediately began peeling off the bark. Though we did not have a peeling spud, we improvised with an old shovel that a neighbor loaned us. It had its round tip cut off an inch from the end. Its new edge was filed sharp to cut more easily. This proved to be an excellent tool for the purpose (plate 1).

Making a Peeling Spud Out of an Old Shovel

CUT OFF & SHARPEN NEW EDGE

1

The bark stripped off easily because the logs were cut in the early spring when the sap was abundant. But as the weather became warmer we found it increasingly harder to peel the logs, not only because the sap was drying, but because we had no shelter from the hot sun. But worst of all we made the mistake of having our work area downwind from the pig pen.

As we cut and peeled the logs many neighbors came to give us a helping hand and offer us advice. Some of the advice I must admit was rather unsound, but most of it was needed and used.

I started doing labor trades with some of the locals. One neighbor helped me set up batter boards and showed me how to rough out a square 22' x 22'. He checked the square by measuring a line 6' on one side and 8' on its perpendicular. In order for the corner to be an accurate 90-degree angle, the diagonal of the lines had to be 10' long. We measured each corner, then double checked the crossing diagonals. They had less than 1" difference in length (plate 2).

In return for this help I worked on his place with him. Though I didn't know much about construction or farming, I was eager to learn and he was happy to have my help.

It was all valuable learning experience for which I was grateful.

We decided to use ten 24" footings as the primary foundation for the barn. We dug ten holes, one at each corner, one at the center of the sides without doorways and one on each side of the two doorways. Each hole was 12" deep and more than 24" wide. The footings were 24"-high pyramids, 12" square on top graduating to 24"-square at the bottom for maximum support. We made rough 1 x 6 forms and braced them with thin strips of 1x on the outer side. They were each set in one of the holes. I checked the levelness of the forms by filling a hose with water and stretching it from corner-to-corner on one side. The ends of the hose were bent up to just above the tops of the forms. If the forms were level there would be the same space between each hose and the water levels within the hose; in other words, the water levels would each be horizontal with the tops of the forms. If that wasn't the case we would adjust the depths of the forms. If the water level was too high and the hole was filled until the form raised to the height of the others (plate 3).

The cement, gravel, and sand were then measured on a platform, mixed with water

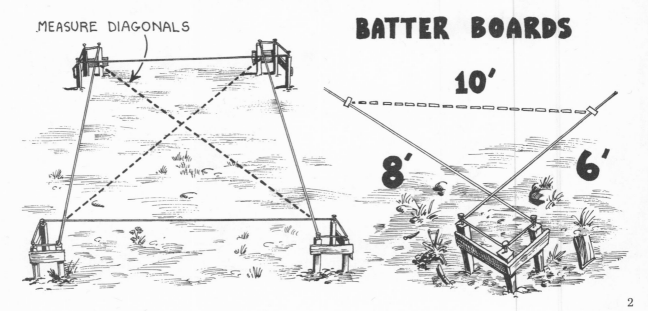

MEASURE DIAGONALS

BATTER BOARDS

10'

8'   6'

2

and poured into the forms. We used a mixture of 1 part Portland Normal Cement, 2 parts gravel, and 3 parts fine sand. We also added quite a few large rocks for volume. This saved on cement and didn't seem to take away from the strength of the footings (plate 4).

Luckily the area for the barn was relatively level so each footing stood between 8″-to-12″ above ground. The sill logs would rest on top of these footings.

We figured that the best floor for a barn is a natural one of porous soil. Urine seeps through it and after a season or two the decaying bedding and uncollected manure break down on it and produce an excellent humus top soil which can later be put into the garden. There is one problem which arises though when building a log structure

3

FOUNDATION POSTS

HOSE LEVEL

WHEN WATER IS SAME HEIGHT AT BOTH HOSE ENDS, IT IS LEVEL

4

MIXING CEMENT

without a floor. All four of the bottom logs are going to be sill logs of the same level. When using any notching method to join logs the logs must be staggered. Two parallel logs should be set on the pillars and two crossing logs should be notched a half log above them. The space between the crossing logs and the center pillars can be filled by making these pillars half a log higher than the others in the beginning. The higher center pillars will then support the raised end logs. The space that is left between those logs and the ground will later be filled with stone work or other foundation material so no additional problems will arise from using this method (plate 5).

Another way to rectify this problem is to make notches in the underside of the two lower logs. These notches should be at least 1/3 of the log's diameter deep and long enough to cover the top of the pillars they will be resting on. Then notch the crossing logs to these with dovetail notches or any other notch you prefer (plate 6).

Dovetail notches are the most popular, used when working with milled or hand-hewn logs because of their interlocking ability. Their design prevents them from coming apart no matter in what direction stress is applied. They pull each wall log toward the center of the building, making it impossible for the logs to fall outward (plate 7). Same holds true when using round logs. Because of this interlocking ability we found it safe to use this notch without having to spike the corners. This saved us money on materials and prevented premature decay in the notches. Nails and spikes contract and expand at different rates than wood. After a

6

CENTER POST SLIGHTLY HIGHER TO COMPENSATE FOR START OF STAGGER

5

period of time, the moisture and oxidation which collects between the two surfaces will rot the wood and weaken the corners.

Dovetail notches are simple to make. First I used a level to find two parallel lines (north-to-south) at each end of the log. The lines were about 1″-to-1½″ in from the outer circumference of the log end (plate 8). Then I measured the diameters of the crossing logs which will be notched above. I marked these measurements on the side of the prospective ends of the lower sill logs.

A sharp pruning saw was used to cut in against the grain to meet the depth of the parallel lines (plate 9). With an old axe head and a hammer, each of the pieces was knocked out (plate 10). The log was then placed in position.

I rested a square on the end of this log and slanted it at a slight angle then marked a line across the log end. A saw cut was made at the rear of the notch to the same depth of the slanted line (plate 11). This piece was then knocked out and a wedge-shaped log end was formed to interlock with a coupling notch (plate 12).

7

8

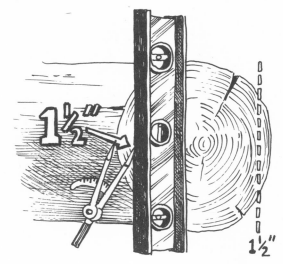

9

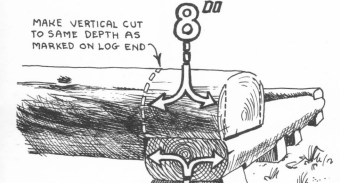

MAKE VERTICAL CUT TO SAME DEPTH AS MARKED ON LOG END

10

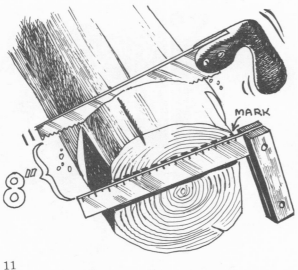

11

12

13

A crossing log was put in position above the first logs. The level was again used to find two parallel lines and the appropriate pieces were sawed and knocked out. As the top log was held in position, I rested a square on the slant of the bottom-log notch and measured the distance between the high and low points. The distance and slant were duplicated on the side of the upper-log notch with the high point being at about half of the log's diameter. A line was drawn, a saw cut was made against the grain, and the piece was chopped out with a hatchet (plates 13 and 14).

The log was then fitted into place, which usually meant hewing its bottom until it fit snugly. The amount of hewing needed with a relatively straight log depends on how carefully the slants and distances of the log below were measured. If care was taken it would fit tightly without any hewing. That was seldom the case. If the notch was cut too deeply, the log bottoms and tops would have to be hewed accordingly until the notch interlocked properly. If the notch was not cut deep enough and the gap between the logs is too wide, then the bottom notch should be hatcheted or axed out until it is widened enough for proper fit. This process was repeated until the walls were finished (plate 15 and 16).

Since we were lucky enough to have plenty of good logs to choose from, we built the barn walls out of solid logs wherever possible. But since I miscounted the number we needed, because I didn't cut an over abundance to compensate for error, we ended up not having enough long logs for the whole structure. The back wall was consequently constructed of 8½'-long pieces. An 8½' piece on either side left room for a 5' doorway in the center.

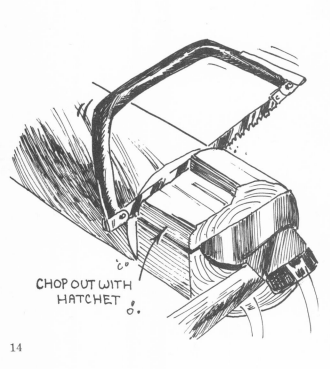

CHOP OUT WITH
HATCHET

14

16

15

If notch is cut too deep, the log will keep the joint from fitting

correct error by hewing along length of log...

...joint drops into snug fit

Though the logs were heavy tamarack which had dried for less than two months, they were not very difficult to lift. Using a simple parbuckle, my wife and I managed to hoist most of them in place, and waited for visitors to assist us with the others. The parbuckle consisted of a long section of rope with both ends tied around the sill or any low log. The center of the rope was brought to the inside of the building, thrown over the wall, and looped around a log which was placed at the foot of the two skids that leaned against the wall. As the rope was again pulled to the inside, it raised the log on the skids and hoisted it to the top (see chapter 4).

We spiked the fitted logs on either side of the doorways to keep them in place when openings were later sawed through. Some builders spike either side of the window areas too, but we felt that would limit us in window design.

We notched in a crossbeam above the walls before we placed the top wall logs in. This way the top wall log would be fitted over the pole to seat it snugly. The crossbeam is necessary structurally because it supports the ceiling joists which hold up the loft floor and make an additional tie-in for the walls.

The joists were then put in. Each was placed at 19″ center except for the one at the rear. There we allowed a 30″ space between that joist and the rear wall for a trap door. This trap door is an inside entrance to the hay loft. It is large enough to easily allow hay bales to be thrown down through it for the hungry occupants waiting below (plate 17).

At this point we finally located a portable cement mixer we could borrow for a day. A fellow up the road, who eventually became a good friend, needed the use of my truck, so in trade he loaned me the mixer for a day. That

17

18

entire day, until late that evening, my wife and I mixed many loads of cement and gathered many large rocks to build a stone retaining wall around the bottom of the barn. Before the night was finished a very solid and beautiful secondary foundation was completed by lamp light. This retaining wall prevented any sagging of logs and sealed in the sections between the footings (plate 18).

Next came the roof. We chose to use a typical gambroled roof because that style provided the most usable storage space for hay and grain. The first frame was constructed 14' wide, 7' high, and 22' long from front-to-rear. This space proved to be more than adequate for at least four tons of hay and many sacks of grain. We used 5"-to-6" diameter poles for the frame and reinforced it with centerposts, side braces, and

19

DETAIL OF
LOOKOUT
CONSTRUCTION

double criss-crossed poles at front and rear. I found from seeing many old barns with collapsed roofs and still strong walls, that you cannot overbuild the roof section. It needs all the support you can give it (plates 19 and 20).

After the frame was secured, a ridgepole complete with notches for a second set of braces was placed above it. The braces and a top ridgepole were then spiked in.

We cut 24 poles which were 4″-to-5″ diameter to a length of 8′ for the lower set of rafters. The bottoms of these poles were notched and spiked into either end of the 12 cross beams. The tops were attached to the top of the frame. After these rafters were in place, 24 more were cut. Three vertical sections, each 4′ in height, were set in the notches at the front, center, and rear of the ridgepole. We braced them and wondered how to hoist the final ridgepole. My wife was pregnant, and we thought it unwise for her to chance the chore. Before long though her cousin and his massive friend came for a visit. Without even being asked, the friend checked out the situation, carried the ridgepole to the roof and hoisted it up. He then slammed the spikes in place and helped us connect the other rafters.

I examined the framework and decided that the pitch of the top rafters looked too awkward because of their height. We removed the few connecting rafters, chainsawed 1′ from each of the three extensions, and sledge hammered the excess pieces from the ridgepole. We later replaced it and followed the friend's suggestion of enjoying a few beers for the remainder of the afternoon. A few inches were later cut off the upper rafters to compensate for the shortened extensions, and they were again spiked into place (plate 21).

20

21

In Harmony with Nature   179

Thus far, building expenses had been nominal. They were less than $80, including cost of feed for the neighbor's pig. But at that point, milled lumber was needed, unless we wanted to rip 1x's out of available logs. My lack of skill with the chain saw prevented any further thought on the matter.

Shopping for usable, but inexpensive lumber can be a big chore. We went from mill-to-mill to find enough economy-grade material to floor the hay loft and use as nailers over the rafters. Lumber prices are constantly on the increase. Even the lowest grade 1x's we found were over our budget. We finally located a private party who was selling his stash. It included enough 1 x 8 and 1 x 10 cedar, at $40 per-thousand-board-feet, to do our flooring and enough other 1x to use for nailers and gable ends.

The tops of the ceiling joists had to be hewn before the loft floor could be laid. After the hewing, cedar boards were quickly nailed across the joists and a space was left for the trap door. The nailers were then attached to the lower rafters. It was not until after they were attached that we found out it was not necessary to construct a solid covering. We then spaced the upper nailers 6" apart to save labor and materials.

We considered many different roof coverings, and although it was decided that a cedar shake roof would have been the most aesthetic and least expensive, we chose to use an aluminum roof. The shake roof would have been impractical because of snow buildup on the upper sections and difficulty of climbing on it in the middle of winter to clean it off. A freak mid-September snowfall reinforced our decision. The barn needed a roof immediately. The cost of the aluminum roofing was $100, but it was worth it. Though it lacks natural beauty, it is the most durable and maintenance

free of possible materials. It also sheds snow and is easy to install. Two of us put most of it up in a day. It was late November before it snowed again (plate 22).

Now, it was time for the interior work to begin. And it was time for the barn to have doors and windows. I measured where I wanted to have the front door and nailed up 2 x 4's as vertical guides for my chainsaw cuts. Then I cut through the logs to make the opening. That opening was framed with a double thickness of 2 x 6 which acted as hinge supports and door frame. It took me a while to figure out what design of door I wanted. I needed a solid door for weather, but I did not want a massive door that would be too heavy for the hinges. I looked through the scrap pile of log pieces that I had left over and found some short sections of 4"-to 5" diameter cedar and tamarack. So I set up a guide, using a 2 x 8 platform with two nails sticking out of it spaced about 3" apart. The log pieces were each cut to 38" because I decided it would be nice to have dutch doors for ventilation and light. I hammered a log section down onto the nails of the platform and made it stand upright as I ripped it down the middle with the chainsaw. This process was quick and easy.

After the half rounds were cut they were laid out in a line. I alternated the tamarack and cedar for appearance and structural reasons. Nails seem to hold better in tamarack, so I made sure to space them. The cedar backing was then nailed on and one door was ready for hinging.

The second one was done in the same manner and apple wood handles were added as a finishing touch. We are very satisfied with the way the doors came out (plates 23–25).

22

WWRRAAAA

2"x8"

36"

23

2"x8" FRAME

LCLCCLCL

BACKING OF LIGHT CEDAR 1'x

½ ROUND SLABS OF ALTERNATING CEDAR AND LARCH WOOD

24

25

DOOR LATCH

2" x 4"s

1" x 6"

HEMLOCK
1" x 6" BOARDS

BUILDING PAPER

26

27

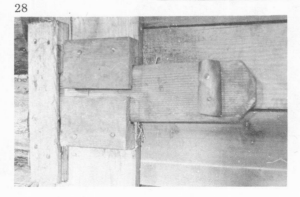

28

We framed the rear doorway and the hayloft doorway and decided to make those doors differently. They were made of three layers of 1 x 6 hemlock and one layer of black building paper sandwiched in as a protective vapour barrier. The first layer of hemlock was of short horizontal boards which were laid out on a flat surface. These boards were covered with the building paper. A layer of vertical 1x6's was placed over the paper and nailed to the bottom layer. A final diagonal piece and borders were added for support (plates 26–28).

The window spaces were next to be dealt with. I wanted to make sure the occupants of this building had plenty of light, but I knew I had to safeguard against window breakage, especially with our onerous animals. After searching through many of the junked cars in the area I found some nearly rectangular glass in a few early model Dodges and DeSotos. This safety glass was easy to install and is very difficult to shatter (plate 29).

We paneled the hayloft gables with the cedar 1x and wanted to begin working on the interior (none too soon). The weather was getting colder and the animals were still without shelter. But instead of starting on the barn's interior, we were forced to construct a root cellar immediately because the frost was already destroying our pumpkins and winter squash. The root cellar did not take long to build once we got into it.

On completion of that project a friend of ours saw the barn, praised it, and asked us if we wanted to take care of his milking cow while he and his family went away for the winter. Fresh milk and butter, homemade cheeses, ice cream, and yogurt; what homesteader could refuse such treats. He and his family planned to leave in two weeks. Though our black angus was not giving milk yet, she would one day, so one of the stalls was designed to house his cow.

After figuring out the various stall sizes, we dug holes in the ground a foot deep to bury the bottoms of the upright supports. Their tops were notched and spiked into the above ceiling joists. The size of the stall depended on the animal it housed. The two identical stalls at the right front were built to house the heifers or meat steers of the year. Those stalls are about 5′ wide and 8′ long. Each contains a feeding manger and an area for a water bucket. They have crisscrossed log gates which hinge and latch to the upright supports (plate 30).

Behind them we constructed a 10′ x 8′ goat stall sufficient to house two or three goats. It contains a feeding manger and a bucket area in one section and a milking platform with feeder in the other. The horizontal dividers as well as the gate's cross pieces are spaced less than 4″ apart and are over 6′ high. They will be higher yet because goats are clever little devils, especially the ones we have. The goat pen also has a door which opens to a ramp that serves as a walkway to the corral outside. The ramp, when in raised position is also the gate to the corral (plates 31–34).

29

30

31

GOAT STALLS

32

On the other side of the barn we built two more stalls. The 9′ x 5′ front one is for the horse. It is without gate. As long as there is an adequate place on the manger to tie a horse, there is little chance the animal will leave. Cows, on the other hand, should be hooked to a ring, and if possible have gates on their stalls. Our black angus heifer, Beulah, once unhooked herself, got out of her stall, ripped open the milk cow's dairy mash, ate what she wanted, and manured on the rest. When I came in to milk, she ran to the dutch door as the bottom partition closed. She took a leap, came down on that section and flattened it.

The 12′ x 6′ area to the rear is the milking stall. It has a manger and a water-bucket holder. It was built large to give the milker and cow plenty of room while milking (plate 35).

Behind the milk cow's stall is a space about 3½′ x 8′ for storage of a couple bales of hay and a few sacks of grain. There, a ladder goes up to a trap door which serves as inside entrance to the hay loft. A simple pulley-and-rope system was designed to lift and lower the trap door (plate 36–38).

And then came chinking. It is a proven fact that the easiest method of chinking a structure is to have a chinking party. Invite all your friends and neighbors to help you and you will complete the chore in one day. We set up a cement mixer and used a mixture of 1 part lime, 1 part masonry cement, and 5 parts clean, fine sand. When I rechink the walls after they have a chance to settle I will just use masonry cement and sand (1 part-to-3 parts) because too much lime causes the mixture to be less durable. Masonry cement already has lime in it.

We made palettes out of pieces of plywood and supplied each helper with

Goat Area

33

34

35

36

HOLE DRILLED
THRU BOARDS

FLOOR JOIST

INWOODS '74

PEG TO TIE
OFF PULLEY

37

38

a palette, an inexpensive pair of rubber gloves (to prevent lime burns), all the food they could eat, and all the wine punch they could drink. First we hammered in many nails along the top of the logs. They were spaced about 2″ apart and were bent in toward the building so they could hold in the chinking.

I controlled the mixer and could never keep up with the enthusiastic workers. The work went well, but I noticed that as the huge punch bowl emptied, the chinking got sloppier. That didn't matter though. The following day after sleeping off our hangovers my wife, a friend, and I went over the walls with a wire brush and a whisk broom to level the sections which protruded. We then smoothed out the rough surfaces. The chinking should not have ridges sticking out from the logs. It should be concave and should blend into the wood. This prevents water from collecting on it and working its way between it and the log, causing premature decay of the walls (plate 39).

With completing the chinking, the barn was almost finished (plate 40). All that was left to do was repair Beulah's damages.

It has been over a year now since we completed the barn. We are very happy with it and we are proud of our achievement. I sometimes think back at the pleasure I had when building it. Each problem and each hassle that was overcome gave me a little more confidence and reinforced my belief in this type of life. Every time a neighbor or a friend wanders up to offer his help or every time someone makes a useful suggestion to us a new-born faith in my fellow man grows stronger and becomes more a part of me. Every time I work with someone whether it be on their project or mine, I learn a little more about communicating my own needs because I become more in touch with them as I experience them. More and more I'm realizing that the only way to be successfully self-sufficient, without the need of an established order, is to cooperate and communicate with those around who also want to live the good life. Its surprising how many of us there are.

39

40

A Sheltering Arch

With our primary shelter, the house finished, it was time to think about the other buildings we needed. The goats and horses were comfortable in the small, old barn, but there was not enough space in there to store all the hay that was need for them. It looked like it was going to be a fine year for crops and we knew we would probably get a few tons of hay from our own fields. Since the weather in our area is so unpredictable, I knew I could not just leave the freshly cut hay out on the fields to be sun dried, because more often than not an unannounced rain would come down and ruin it all. We needed to have a storage place ready by harvest time.

I thought about different building designs. I wanted a large, open structure that would be both a storage and drying area. It had to have an enclosed loft large enough to store at least 10 tons of baled and loose hay. There were also a lot of tools and equipment around that had no definite places of their own. We needed a place to house all these homeless orphans from the weather.

I decided to build a huge barn-type shelter for everything that needed a home. A 20' x 48' area was prepared and ten concrete piers were poured. They were spaced 12' apart on the 48' sides. Steel pins were then stuck into them to accommodate the hewn 12"-to-14" diameter sill logs which were to stretch along those sides. These long sills are the bottom beams for the 11' upright posts which frame the first story. The posts were spaced 12' on-center above each pier and were notched into the beams. A 48' top-plate beam was then notched above the posts and the posts were braced in place (plate 1).

Wherever beam logs came together over an upright post, that post was shortened and a 24" long log piece was notched in above it to reinforce the joint. The log piece was then spiked to the post and each of the beam sections (plate 2).

This area immediately seemed too small, so we widened it by building on a 12' shed-roofed addition ot the north side, making the barn's width 32'. The new outer wall was framed in the same manner as the other two long sides and its shorter uprights were 8' in height to allow plenty of storage area. Its rafters were spaced at 24" centers, spanning between the beams on either side. Nailing strips were spaced across the rafters and a finish roof of cedar shakes was put on. Thin poles were later run horizontally across the 8' upright posts and scrap 1x sheathing was nailed to them to enclose the shed area. This sheathing shielded the area from direct moisture but did not close it off from the cross currents of wind which allow for good air circulation. This section became ideal for hay drying (plate 3).

To make the racks for the hay, I simply ran smaller 7' rails along each

1

2

3

11′ post of the inner wall and attached them at top and bottom with 4″ spacer blocks. Long spikes, spaced 18″ apart were driven through the rails and into the posts. These spikes act as rungs for the horizontal poles which cross the posts. Five tiers of poles were then extended between the 8′ and 11′ side walls. Their ends rested on the crossing horizontal poles of each wall. During harvest we spread out the freshly cut hay on each tier. When one tier was filled, the poles for the next were put in place. Fresh green hay was then spread out on the second tier, and so on until about an acre of hay was drying over the five racks. After the hay was dry enough to store, the poles were taken down and this 12′ x 48′ section was turned into a winter storehouse for supplies and equipment (plates 4 and 5).

For storage of the hay, the loft area was then constructed. A 48′ log beam was placed over the ends of the shed roof rafters at the 11′ inside wall. The 8″ hewn-log ceiling joists spanned from above that beam to 2′ beyond the top

beam on the south wall. These 22′ joists were spaced at 24″ centers above the side walls. The 2′ that went beyond the beam allowed for a roof eave which would prevent rain and snow from getting into the pen area below. The north side was protected by the shed roof that would be overlapped by the north loft roof eave.

I wanted the loft roof to have steep sides for better drainage. The better the drainage, the less chance of rot because the moisture does not collect on the roof's surface. And, if the roof has a steep pitch, snow slides off before it becomes too heavy. I also wanted the roof to be wide enough to accommodate the several tons of hay our animals would need throughout the long winter months. The common gambroled barn roof interested me but I desired a different design; one that gave even more storage space over the 20′ x 48′ floor area. I thought about the old Navy quonset huts I had been so familiar with. Surely there must be a way to utilize that design when working with logs.

SPACER BLOCKS

SPIKE RUNGS

Hay Drying Racks

4

A framework of log roof braces was constructed over the rough 1x loft floor. The first section was 48'-long, 14'-wide, and 8' in height. The sides were supported by uprights spaced every 12', directly over crossing joists. Also at every 12', a cross beam was notched above the uprights to keep the long framework from spreading. I came down from the loft and examined the framed area. I decided to have the peak of the roof another 4' above it, making the whole barn 24' tall. A sectioned ridgepole that extended 3' past either end of the frame was raised to that height and was braced at 12' intervals by double 12' uprights which spanned between the joists and the peak. These uprights straddled the crossbeams at their centers. They were doubled because each was bracing one end of the four poles which made up the length of the ridgepole. The 48'-long upper purloins were then put in place halfway between the ridgepole and the lower purloins (the lower purloins are the 48' sides of the rectangular roof framework). These purloins also followed the proposed arch of the roof. They were braced by short diagonal boards which straddled each of the crossbeams (plates 6 and 7).

5

7

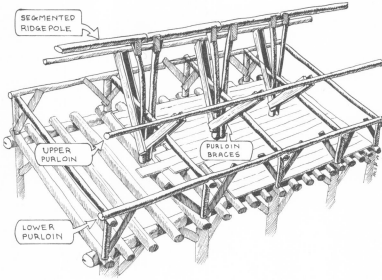

SEGMENTED RIDGEPOLE

UPPER PURLOIN

PURLOIN BRACES

LOWER PURLOIN

6

With the roof supporting frame finished, it was time to put my experiment into action. I found a thick stand of young fir trees and thinned out over 50 saplings which were about 3″ in diameter at the butts. 16′ sections with no large knots were cut from them and were immediately peeled. These sapplings were then put into water to soak for a few days. While they were soaking, I augered a 2″ hole near each end of every other log joist. When the saplings had soaked until they were flexible enough to bend easily, I took one of them out of the water, trimmed its bottom end to 2″, and stuck it into an augered hole. That end was spiked into the joist. The sapling was then bent over the roof frame, and a piece of rope was tied to its top end. That end was pulled down above the ridgepole and the rope was tied to the joist end on the opposite side. The sapling was positioned and nailed to the purloins and the ridgepole. This process was repeated until the rafters were spaced 48″, or two joists, apart on either side of the frame. A pair of longer rafters at either end of the roof, were attached to the top wall beams and were bent forward to the tips of the ridgepole to brace the overhangs (plates 8–10).

For added strength, I decided to put another set of rafters over the ones already in place. To insure a snug fit, the undersides of the top rafters were grooved out about 1″ deep so they cupped over the bottom ones. The grooves were made by a chainsaw with guides on either side of its roller tip bar. The guides were attached to each side of the bar by a bolt which came through the roller tip opening. The diagonal guides straddled either side of the pole, allowing the chainsaw to cut a 1″ groove in it. To make the groove, I dogged a pole across two logs, stood over it, and

cut down its length at a slight right angle. I then made a left angle cut deep enough to meet the first cut and removed the piece in between (plate 11).

These top rafters were nailed above the bottom ones and the rafter ends were cut a few inches after they met the ridgepole, allowing each set to cross at the peak. After the rafters were all in place, a second ridge pole was put in over the crossing ends to sandwich them in. It was spiked to the rafter ends and bolted to the bottom ridgepole with 3/8″ bolts at 6′ intervals.

The ridgepole sections that stuck out beyond the end rafters were reinforced by a third piece that was wedged in between the top and bottom ridgepole ends. Before that third piece was bolted in, two holes were drilled into either end of the bottom pole to accomodate two "U"-bolts from which large pulleys would hang.

FIR

8

9

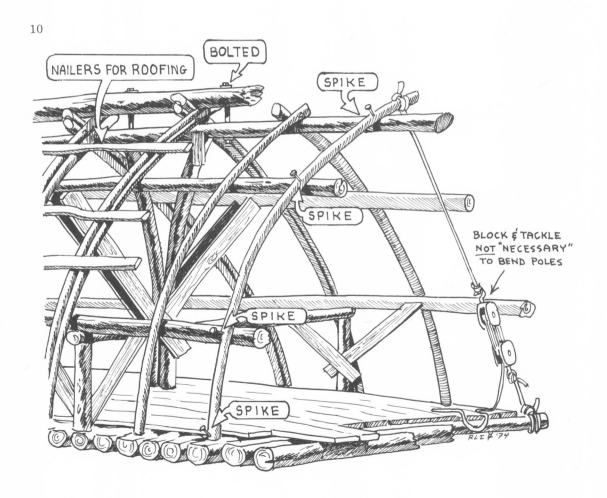

Next came the nailers for the cedar shake finish roof. These nailers are 3"-to-4" diameter poles which I hewned on two sides with a sharp broad axe, making flat surfaces for the shakes to be nailed to. I prefer to do my hewing in the winter. For some reason all types of wood split faster and cleaner when they are frozen. For example, try splitting a birch round in the middle of the winter, then try splitting that same birch round at spring thaw. You will notice an amazing difference.

I used the snakiest, most crooked poles for the nailers because it is not necessary for shakes to be nailed to a straight strip, as long as they have a nice flat surface. These nailers were spaced anywhere from 18"-to-20" apart for the 26" cedar shakes. Because of the steep roof pitch, it was not necessary to put the nailers any closer since the shakes do not have to overlap as much as they would on a roof with a less steep pitch. This also saves on shakes (plates 12 and 13).

The homemade shakes were attached to the nailers (see Chapter 6). The gable ends of the loft area were then sheathed in with 8'-long slabs which were being discarded at a local railroad tie mill. Double doors were framed on the front gable through which hay bales would be brought in. On each gable, a ventilation opening was left directly under the roof overhang to prevent the stored hay from mildewing (plates 14 and 15).

Just like the house, the barn was built slowly and carefully. I take great pride in my work, especially when I am building for myself. And as I mentioned before, we found a piece of land to our liking and we plan to live on it for a long time to come, so whatever we do on it has to be done right. Our buildings have to be aesthetically pleasing as well as practical; our gardens and fields have to be neat and straight; our landscape has to be trimmed and well cared for; even our fences have to accentuate the natural beauty which surrounds us (plate 16 and 17). Our homestead is a reflection of our own personalities; we respect it as we respect ourselves.

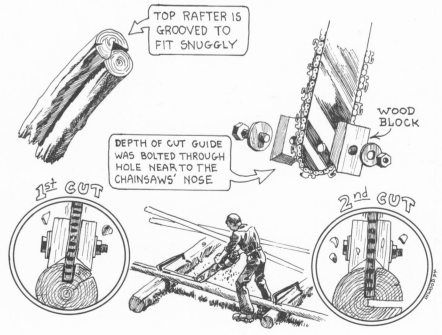

TOP RAFTER IS GROOVED TO FIT SNUGGLY

WOOD BLOCK

DEPTH OF CUT GUIDE WAS BOLTED THROUGH HOLE NEAR TO THE CHAINSAWS' NOSE

1st CUT

2nd CUT

11

12

13

14

15

16

17

Hand Hewn Gate

INWOOD '73

1

Since we needed a place where we could cleanse and rejuvenate ourselves as we planned and developed our new homestead, one of the first and most important buildings which we constructed was the sauna. I personally do not like tub baths because bathing in a tub of still water doesn't really get you clean. Bacteria remains in still water and coats your skin with an oily film, thus you are never really rid of the dirt you entered with. A sauna cleanses your skin of its surface dirt as well as ridding your body of its inner impurities. It also helps you unwind after a hard day of working and provides you with a warm, peaceful chamber to meditate in.

A sauna cleanses you from the inside out by flushing your blood with its heat. This stimulates your sweat glands to exude their juices, which wash through your pores as they flow outward to cool your skin. Then after your body is saturated with sweat and you can not stand anymore heat, you scrub down with soap and plunge into a pool of cold water or stand under a cold shower and rinse off. The cooling effect of the water momentarily stimulates you and closes your pores. Afterward, when you reenter the sauna or go to another place to relax, you will find that the previous combination of stifling heat and cold shock induces restfulness and loosens muscular and nervous tension.

Saunas have other healthful advantages which are beneficial to country living. They help heal surface wounds by bringing blood to afflicted areas. They act as vaporizers to clear out stuffy sinuses for sufferers of head colds (cold plunges or showers are not recommended after this treatment. They relieve party hangovers because they work out all the alcoholic toxins from your body by stimulating circulation. Saunas are also conducive for massages and are a great place to get to know people (plate 1).

I built my sauna into a hillside, close to where I planned to build my house. It was set into the hill to make full use of the insulative property of the earth. My design called for many of the precautions mentioned in Chapter 5 to make sure that it would be well protected from runoff. I dug out a hole, 9½'-wide, 11'-long, and 5'-deep for the structure—all by hand. This, needless to mention, was a tedious task that took several weeks to complete. But I did not want heavy machinery leaving its destructive scars on my land. I desired a hole this size because I wanted to make sure the sauna would be large enough to accommodate six-to-eight people, but small enough to retain heat well. Many of the people I know have saunas which are 8 x 8. That space seemed too small to me because it only allows a few bathers to be far enough away from the source of heat to not be scorched by it.

The dirt I shoveled out of the hole went to the downhill side of the sauna site for the plunge. It was prevented from going any further down the hillside by four upright posts with crossing boards. The ends of the posts were buried into the ground and the boards were nailed across them to hold the dirt. On the uphill side the ground was leveled so the runoff would have a tendency to flow down the sides of the hill instead of draining in back of the sauna (plate 2).

Since this sauna was to be my practice building, I wanted to experiment with many different techniques in it. I wanted to become familiar with them through practice, then later choose which mediums I preferred working with, to incorporate them into our house. The walls were framed with post-and-beam and were filled with dimension lumber, cement, and a stucco mixture.

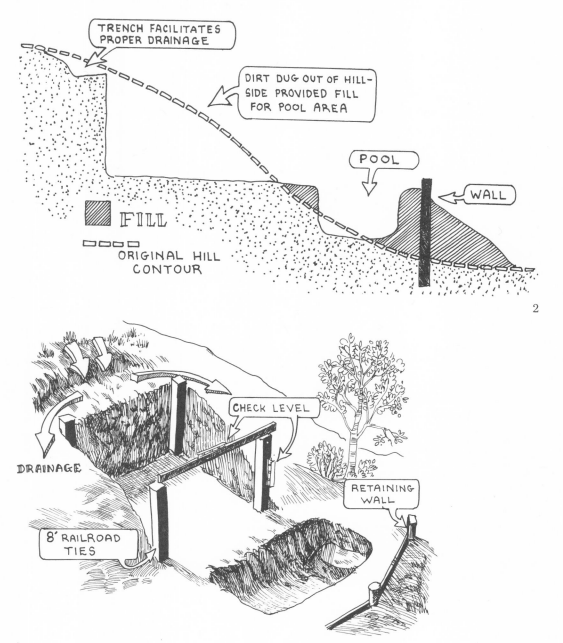

TRENCH FACILITATES PROPER DRAINAGE

DIRT DUG OUT OF HILLSIDE PROVIDED FILL FOR POOL AREA

POOL

WALL

FILL

ORIGINAL HILL CONTOUR

2

DRAINAGE

CHECK LEVEL

RETAINING WALL

8' RAILROAD TIES

3

To start them, I dug four corner holes in the 9½ x 11 trench. Each was 3'-deep and wide enough to accommodate an end of a creosoted railroad tie. These 8'-long railroad ties were discards which I bought for 25 cents each. They are excellent to use when in contact with the earth, because they were thoroughly soaked in creosote and will not rot out for at least as long as I'll be around to use the sauna.

After burying the bottom ends of the upright ties 3' into the ground so their top ends would be flush with the uphill side of the hole, I ran 2 x 4's above each of them and made sure, with a carpenter's level, they were all the same height. I then packed sand and gravel around them and plumbed them on two sides with the same instrument (plate 3).

The front uprights were temporarily held together with 2 x 4's so they would stay in place while I dug an 18"-deep trench between them. This trench was for a short retaining wall. The wall would extend from the bottom of the trench to 12" above ground. Spikes were driven into the sides of the uprights and 1x forms were then nailed between the ties. They were braced every 3' with narrow slats. Holes were drilled into these slats and lengths of baling wire were run between them on either side. The wire ends were then wrapped around nails to hold them in place. These braces effectively prevented the forms from bulging as we poured in the cement. The mixture we used was 5 parts sand, 1 part Portland Cement, and as many flat rocks as we could put into the mortar without weakening it (plate 4).

WIRE SUPPORTS PREVENT BOWING

12"

STAKES HOLD BOTTOM FORM BOARD STRAIGHT

3'

18"

4

The two side retaining walls were dealt with next. These walls were built to a height of 2½', using square rocks which we trucked in from wherever they were available. They were mortared in without forms. Whenever you build such a wall it is important that you use flat, wide rocks which stack up well. 10″ channels were dug between the side uprights, and spikes were nailed along them to tie the walls together. A 4″ layer of mortar, 3 parts sand, and 1 part masonry cement, was poured into the channels for the bottom rocks to set into. The remaining wall rocks were mortared in above them until the walls were built to height, then they were checked for levelness with crossing 2 x 4's (plate 5).

Above the upright posts, I put in a double-layer top plate of interlocking horizontal logs. These logs were 10″ cedars that were peeled and ready. They brace the long, overhanging roof and raise the walls another 18″. The first layer of side logs was notched over the uprights. The crossing logs were then round-notched onto the side logs. To make my notches, I eyeballed the contour of the lower logs, figured the approximate depth and width of the notch, and marked that estimation on the log to be notched. Then, with a swede saw I cut deep scores into the notch area to the drawn outline and knocked the pieces out with a chisel (*see* Chapter 1). The upper layer was notched over the first in the same manner. The top side logs are 17′ long,

extending 2′ beyond the rear wall and 4′ beyond the front wall to support the roof's overhangs.

At this point, because the weather was getting cold and rainy, we decided to put on the sheltering roof instead of filling in the walls. I figured out a comfortable pitch for the roof and spiked in two 18″ upright ridgepole supports above the front and rear top wall plates. These uprights allowed the roof a slight pitch of less than 15 degrees. I didn't want the pitch any higher because heat would be more apt to escape through the higher roof. I also planned to finish the roof with sod. If it was any steeper than 15 degrees, the loose sod would have more of a tendency to erode off of it.

A 17′-long ridgepole was notched over the short uprights and the rafters were seated deep into the top side plates and the ridgepole. These six rafter sets were each spaced at 36″ on-center. I lap-notched them deeply to make them level with the tops of the side logs and the ridgepole. This eliminated having to use spacers between each rafter to fill in the usual gap between the subroof and top wall plates (plate 6).

The lap joints were easy to make. I simply sawed and chiseled out the square laps at 36″ intervals on the side plates and ridgepole. I then figured the angle for the rafter top by resting the rafter bottom above the side plate so the top met with the ridgepole. I eyeballed the angle and sawed into the

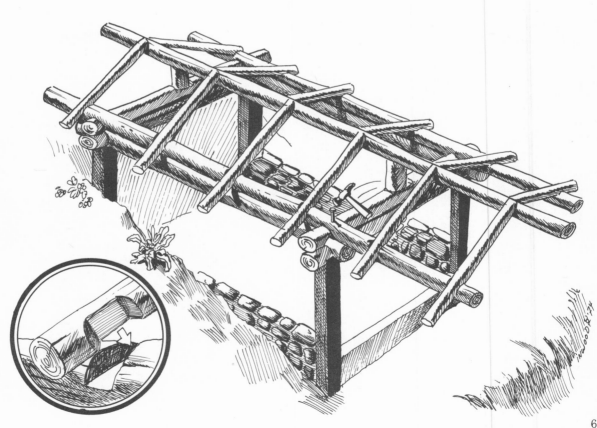

6

rafter top. After spiking it into the side of the ridgepole, I then eyeballed the angles and depths of the bottom cuts in the same manner. If I were to seat the rafters again, I would just slightly hew the sides of the ridgepole instead of notching them. The deep notches weakened the structural soundness of that primary beam (plate 7).

Because of the heavy sod roof that would be above it, I made sure to construct a strong, vapour proof subroof. The first layer was of 2 x 8 cedar boards which were nailed lengthwide across the rafters. Over those boards was a layer of heavy building paper and another layer of 2 x 8's which crossed the first. Thin strips of fiberglas insulation were stuffed between both sides of the peak and over the sidewall plates to seal off these areas. Then a ridgecap of aluminum flashing was put over the boards to detour the rain from entering through the peak gap.

To seal this subroof, I spread melted tar over the top boards with an old broom. The tar came in 100-pound lugs which I melted down in an old bucket. I needed 200 pounds to initially cover my roof, a cost of $14. Another thin coating will go on it when I spread the coarse gravel. This gravel will embed into the soft tar to keep the sod on the roof. Also to hold the sod, 4″ poles were nailed around the outside edge of the roof eaves. They cross at and extend over the peak for an ornamental effect (plate 8).

Even now, without the final sod covering, the sauna roof does not leak at all. When the weather is hot, the uncovered tar has a tendency to get soft and sticky but it doesn't drip or run. The only problem which did occur with the roof is that the 4′ front overhang which shields the dressing area, sagged under the heavy winter

EYEBALLING THE RAFTER ANGLE

7

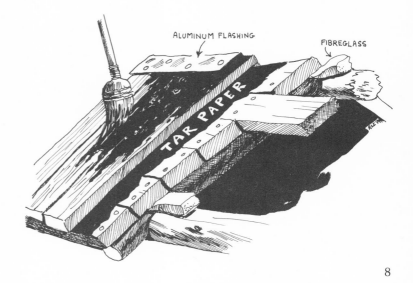

ALUMINUM FLASHING

FIBREGLASS

TAR PAPER

8

9

10

snow load. I corrected that structural problem by notching in two diagonal braces to support the overhang. These braces span from the side plate extensions to the center of the corner upright posts. They have successfully corrected the sag and add a nice aesthetic appeal to the front section (plate 9).

I plan to put 2″-to-3″ of good soil on the roof for the sod covering. It will be seeded with white clover so the roots will help hold the sod together. The flowering clover will make the roof flow into the landscape of the hillside like the first page drawing illustrates.

When the roof was on and the sauna was protected, we returned to the walls, handling each in a different manner. Above the short rock walls on either side, we laid an 8″ strip of fiberglas. A horizontal larch log was placed over each strip and was toe nailed to the corner upright posts. A shallow notch was cut into the center of each of these logs and into the center of the top plate logs above. Two 8 x 8 upright beams were then spiked into these notches. This created four smaller rectangular spaces, two at each side wall. I wanted these smaller spaces because the wood I was using to fill the walls was scrap stuff that was laying around. None of it would go the entire distance between the corner posts.

The outside edge of each of these rectangular areas was framed with 2 x 2 nailing strips and three of the four sections were filled in with horizontal 4x planks. The fourth rectangular section was divided again with two 4 x 4 uprights. These uprights support the small hewn poles which framed an 8″ x 10″ window (plate 10).

To brighten the outer rectangular sections of the side walls and give them a rammed-earth effect, the spaces created by the 2 x 2 nailing strips were filled with a stucco like mixture. To prepare the sections, I stapled in a double thickness of chicken wire in each of the areas framed by the 2 x 2 nailers. The thickness closest to the inner wall was ¼″ away from the paneling; the outer one was about 1″ away from it. The strips were also lined with several bent, rusty nails to hold the stucco mortar in place. The mixture I used was the basic 3-part sand, 1-part masonry cement, mixture. The sand was a fine river bottom type. It was mixed dry so there would be less chance of shrinkage. I added water until the mortar was a paste-like and maleable consistency. I worked it into the chicken wire until it covered it and came out to the edge of the uprights. I was able to build up this thickness in a one-day period instead of applying it in several coats as stucco is usually dealt with.

Burlap was hung over the stuccoed wall and the drying mortar was sprayed with water for several days to cure it and prevent it from setting up too early. It set up well without obvious shrinking or cracking and the wall spaces were sealed in efficiently (plate 11).

Many artistic touches can be added to the stucco as it is drying. It can be drawn or painted on, or pieces of colorful glass can be embedded into it to beautify the building (plate 12).

To fill in the front section, I first laid burlap on top of the short retaining wall. The burlap acts as a gasket to prevent air from whizzing between the retaining wall and the 6 x 8 horizontal beam which was toenailed in over it. This beam provided a bottom wood surface for the 8 x 8's which were to frame the doorway. These uprights broke the front wall area into three rectangles, the middle one being the entrance to the sauna. The other two areas were framed with 2 x 4's that were nailed to the centers of the surrounding burlap lined beams. Rough cut 1x sheathing was then nailed to the outsides of the 2 x 4#, closing off these two rectangular sections.

A layer of building paper was tacked on to the inside of the 2 x 4's and an inner sheathing of 2 x 6's was nailed over it. A small area was left open near the top of the inside wall to allow sawdust insulation to be shoved in between the walls. This sawdust was packed down as tight as possible so it

LOTS OF OLD BENT NAILS

DOUBLED OVER WIRE MESH

.STUCCO.
MIX
1 PART MASONRY CEMENT
3 PARTS VERY FINE SAND
Water
AS LITTLE AS POSSIBLE~ BUT ENOUGH FOR A WORK- ABLE, PLASTIC CONSISTENCY

INWOOD '74

11

wouldn't have a tendency to settle. After the sawdust was packed in, the top sheathing boards were nailed in place (plate 13).

The center 32" x 48" entranceway was then framed in and a door of 2 x 6 tongue-and-groove cedar was hinged in place. These cedar boards were held together with 2 x 4's which were doweled into them at top and bottom (plate 14).

The back wall had to be structurally sound and able to repel any drainage that would come in from the hillside behind it. To create an adequate vapour barrier, I nailed a big sheet of 6 mil plastic between the corner uprights. This vapour shield covered the entire wall section and acted as an outside form to protect the cement wall from the earthen hillside in back of it. The cement and rock portion of the wall was built high enough to shield the blazing heat stove which would be directly in front of it. An 8 x 8 beam was set above the retaining wall, and the remaining upper section was framed and filled with dimensional lumber.

The front and rear gable sections which were created by the roof's pitch were the last areas to be filled in. It took me a while to figure out how I was going to deal with them. I had many ideas but few materials. My decision came at a friend's summer solstice party. There before me, laying all over the field in front of the musician's platform was the material I needed. I collected several cases of the discarded beer bottles and took them home for the sauna gables. The gabled areas were prepared with chicken wire strips which I stapled from the top plate log to the underside of the subroof boards in a zig-zag pattern. Bent nails were then added to also grip the mortar.

The chicken wire not only held the concrete, but it also stabilized the large

number of bottles as they were being cemented in. The job was simple and went very well. The setting mortar was sprayed with water for about a week to prevent it from drying too fast or cracking. The end result was and still is a beautiful amber light shining in through many tightly cemented bottle bottoms (plate 15).

I began the interior by laying a floor of shale. The shale pieces that made up this floor were 1'-to-2' slabs, ½"-to-1½" thick, which were outcroppings from a hillside in an area where this kind of rock occurs. Before I laid the shale mosaic pattern, the floor area was first prepared with a 3" thickness of sand for the slabs to set into. The spaces between them were then mortared over so the sand would not get on people's feet (plate 16).

Something I noticed about other saunas that annoyed me was when people would run in and out, to plunge and return, they would let so much heat out that it would uncomfortably lower the temperature of the room and even cause drafts. I remedied this problem in mine by building a framed-in entry chamber to absorb the temperature change. This area is only 2'-long and the width of the doorway, but it works well. To frame this area I set up two upright poles for the inside corners. I figured as long as interior uprights were being set up, they might as well have some structural significance. I ran a horizontal rafter brace between two rafters on either side of the area and notched the uprights under them to hold them in place. This produced an extra support for a large section of the heavy sod roof. Horizontal poles were then nailed across the uprights, just above the top of the doorway. These poles created a ledge above the entrance chamber. A horizontal pole, spanning

12

13

14

16

between the side walls, was put in to continue the ledge to these walls. 1¾″ slats were then notched into this horizontal pole on either side of the chamber ceiling. This raised platform is for people who like super hot saunas.

The outer chamber itself was then walled and ceilinged with 1x boards which spanned from the inside posts to the narrow nailing strips that framed the doorway. A floor was put in this area so there would be two gradual 6″ steps into the sauna instead of one drastic step (plates 17–19).

Two vertical bench ledges were nailed to the back wall just above its 2½′-high cement section. An end of each of the inside horizontal bench supports was nailed above them. These bench supports span from the rear wall to the front wall and were notched into the entrance chamber uprights so they wouldn't have to span that entire distance unbraced. A 2 x 4 was then run along each side wall just above the cement retaining walls. They were approximately level

BEER BOTTLE MASONRY

STRIPS OF TWISTED CHICKENWIRE

INWOOD '74

15

17

18

19

with the inside bench poles and provided a shelf for the outside end of the 1¾″ bench slats. The inside ends were notched into the horizontal support and their tops were trimmed with a saw so there were no rough edges sticking out.

These slats were spaced 1″ apart to allow heat to come up from underneath and circulate around the whole body of the bather. These spaces also provided an area where the excess moisture can drip off their sweat soaked bodies instead of them having to sit or lay in the wetness. I might change the slat design of the upper platform because bathers on the lower benches sometimes complain about such drippings. Also, diagonal boards can be fitted between the slats so the bathers can lean against them at a comfortable angle.

This sauna is heated by a super-duper homemade 15-gallon barrel wood heater, designed and built especially for the structure by a close friend. It sits on top of a cradle of 4″ poles which is surrounded and covered with rocks to help it reflect heat out into the sauna. The stove's chimney goes straight up through the roof, rather than making a bend into the wall. I think this is a safer method because there is no chance of creosote collecting in the bending areas and creating chimney fire. When creosote builds up in a straight pipe, this pipe can be cleaned out from above without having to be taken apart. The sooty deposits will fall back into the stove and burn again. To keep creosote buildup down, burn dry wood, and let a lot of air circulate through the fire box.

Where the chimney goes through the ceiling, it is reinforced with a 36″ length of Yukon-type, double-walled galvanized pipe. This pipe has a 4″ dead air space between the walls for protection. I filled that dead air space with clay to give it more of an insulatory value and packed

additional clay around the stack where it comes out of the roof to seal that opening (plates 20–22).

We throw water on the rocks to create steam for a hotter, wet vapour bath. The sauna is large enough for the bathers to be a comfortable distance away from the stove so they won't get roasted by its radiant heat. I personally like to start off dry and after a while, throw a lot of water on the stove to fill the room with steam. This steam raises the temperature level and induces me to sweat until all my pores are saturated. Soon my body can't stand anymore of the stifling heat. Then I run outside, jump in the plunge, and stay in the cold water until that too becomes uncomfortable, and I repeat the process till I feel totally clean and relaxed.

We have been using a temporary cooling device until the plunge is completed. It is a showerhead connected to an upright pole. It is fed by a plastic water pipe that runs down from a nearby mountain creek.

Saunas can be used for other purposes beside bathing, massaging, and getting to know people. We use ours for a fruit drying shed during harvest time. Since harvest time in this area is after the short, hot summer, we cannot leave the apples, apricots, and plums out to dry. Instead, we put the fruit on screen racks and keep the wood heater going for a few days until all the fruit is dried. A sauna is also a handy place to dry clothes when the weather is foul and there are no facilities for that purpose around.

We enjoy our sauna and have had many compliments on its design. It is comfortable, spacious, and heat seems to distribute very well throughout it. Even with six or eight bathers, it is not too crowded, yet it is easy to keep hot.

When the sauna was first completed

21

we used to bathe in it as many as three or more times a week. We soon noticed that we were getting dehydrated and seemed to always be thirsty. It is unhealthy to take so many saunas in such a short time because the heat pulls out too much moisture from your body. We found that one a week is sufficient and is best for health.

While on the subject of precautions, I want to mention a couple more hints. Do not eat immediately before a sauna because the high temperature speeds up your heart just as heavy exercise does. This overworks your digestive system and makes you nauseous. It is also unhealthy to sauna at the onset of a cold because the shock of the chilly plunge will be too much for such a distressed system to take. The sauna itself, followed by a warm rinse instead of a plunge, is beneficial in the later stages of a cold because it clears out nasal stuffiness and cleans out pores.

We are very pleased with the sauna and have been regularly enjoying its health-giving benefits. We consider it a necessary and important structure which should be an intregal part of every natural homestead.

22

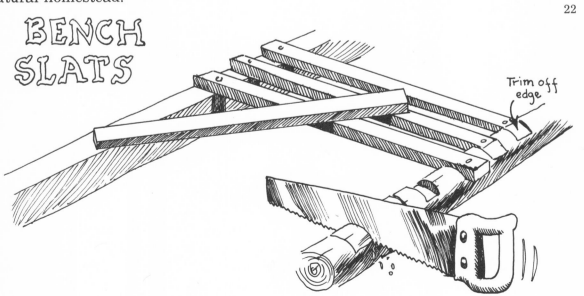

BENCH SLATS

Trim off edge